*Three Observations and
a Dialogue: Round and About SF*

Conversation Pieces

A Small Paperback Series from Aqueduct Press

Subscriptions available: www.aqueductpress.com

About the Aqueduct Press Conversation Pieces Series

The feminist engaged with sf is passionately interested in challenging the way things are, passionately determined to understand how everything works. It is my constant sense of our feminist-sf present as a grand conversation that enables me to trace its existence into the past and from there see its trajectory extending into our future. A genealogy for feminist sf would not constitute a chart depicting direct lineages but would offer us an ever-shifting, fluid mosaic, the individual tiles of which we will probably only ever partially access. What could be more in the spirit of feminist sf than to conceptualize a genealogy that explicitly manifests our own communities across not only space but also time?

Aqueduct's small paperback series, Conversation Pieces, aims to both document and facilitate the "grand conversation." The Conversation Pieces series presents a wide variety of texts, including short fiction (which may not always be sf and may not necessarily even be feminist), essays, speeches, manifestoes, poetry, interviews, correspondence, and group discussions. Many of the texts are reprinted material, but some are new. The grand conversation reaches at least as far back as Mary Shelley and extends, in our speculations and visions, into the continually-created future. In Jonathan Goldberg's words, "To look forward to the history that will be, one must look at and retell the history that has been told." And that is what Conversation Pieces is all about.

L. Timmel Duchamp

Jonathan Goldberg, "The History That Will Be" in Louise Fradenburg and Carla Freccero, eds., *Premodern Sexualities* (New York and London: Routledge, 1996)

Published by Aqueduct Press
PO Box 95787
Seattle, WA 98145-2787
www.aqueductpress.com

"Tales of Earth: Terraforming in Recent Women's Science Fiction."
Foundation: International Journal of Science Fiction, Reading, UK. Spring
(2000): 34-43.

"Third Person Peculiar: Reading Between Academic and SF-
Community Positions in (Feminist) SF." *Femspec: An Interdisciplinary
Feminist Journal*. (2001) 2.1: 74-82.

"Loud Achievements: Lois McMaster Bujold's Science Fiction." *New
York Review of Science Fiction*, No 122, 1+. No 123, 1998. 13-15.

"Letterspace: Letters between Lois McMaster Bujold and Sylvia
Kelso." *Women of Other Worlds: Excursions through Science Fiction and
Feminism*. Eds. Helen Merrick and Tess Williams. Perth: University
of Western Australia, September 1999. 383-409.

Cover Design by Lynne Jensen Lampe
Book Design by Kathryn Wilham
Original Block Print of Mary Shelley by Justin Kempton:
www.writersmugs.com

Cover photo of Pleiades Star Cluster
NASA Hubble Telescope Images, STScI-2004-20
http://hubble.nasa.gov/image-gallery/astronomy-images.html
Credit: NASA, ESA, and AURA/Caltech
Cover photo of Earth
NASA 2002 Blue Marble Series
NASA Goddard Space Flight Center image by Robert Simmon and
Reto Stöckli

ISBN: 978-1-933500-28-7

10 9 8 7 6 5 4 3 2 1

Printed in the USA by Applied Digital Imaging, Bellingham, WA

Conversation Pieces
Volume 24

Three Observations and a Dialogue: Round and About SF

by

Sylvia Kelso

With thanks to my long-suffering PhD supervisor, Professor Robert Dixon, and to Dave Willingham, who published my first fully-fledged academic article. And affectionate and respectful thanks to the many SF writers who over the years have entertained, fascinated, provoked me to thought, and on whose work these speculations were built."

Contents

Third Person Peculiar: Reading Between Academic and SF-Community Positions in (Feminist) SF[1]

A chapter heading in eluki bes shahar's novel *Hell-flower* exactly captures my position here at WisCon, and I'd like to thank her for it. I am somewhat of a third person peculiar at WisCon, and that position, and the tensions between its varying components — as academic researcher, sf reader and/or member of the sf community — is really what this paper is about.

To begin with the most obvious peculiarity, I am an Australian abroad, as you can tell from the moment I talk. To go on, I've always read sf, but though I fit the classic sf reader's profile — first child, introspective, lay interest in science — I have never shared an up-close, personal acquaintance with the sf community, let alone what I understand as fandom, which is the basis of convention-going. I've only glimpsed such a community electronically since a conference about eighteen months ago put me on the Australian sf grapevine and connected me with Justine [Larbalestier] and Helen [Merrick], then fellow post-graduate, or as

1   This essay originated as a paper given at WisCon 20 in Madison, Wisconsin, May 1996.

they say in the US, graduate students. When Justine began mentioning interviews with Connie Willis and meeting Katharine Kerr, my first response was pure sensawunda—like, "Really? WOOWW…" And when Helen and Justine inveigled me onto the Fem-SF listserv, and names like Suzy McKee Charnas and Karen Joy Fowler started turning up on my email, I thought the Inbox had sprouted unicorns.

In another sense, I am even more dislocated in this milieu because I've worked as an academic for the last twelve years, and for at least six of those I have researched, thought, and written about sf. I have read enough rude remarks about how academics mishandle sf to feel dubious about the wisdom of admitting that. And yet I don't really fit the academic slot either, because I don't read "high" fiction for pleasure. For pleasure, I read what I study: feminist (sometimes) detective novels, commercial fantasy, and sf. This sounds simple, but its effect has been more like terraforming. To explain, let me steal a title, in good academic fashion, from a fashionable theorist: I have to talk about the pleasures of the sf text.

In equally feminist fashion, let me use some personal experience here. "Long, long ago, in a galaxy far, far away"—as far away as North Queensland, which is the finger at the eastern side of Australia, and longer ago than I intend to admit—there was a kid sitting on the homestead veranda on a hot January afternoon, reading a book. At least, her body was there; the rest was sneaking across a mysterious sub-Alpine plateau at the head of the Amazon. She read a lot, including a good Children's Encyclopedia, where she had found a beautiful plate of an iguanodon, old style, sitting on its hind-legs like a kangaroo. So she knew what they were, and how they looked, and how long it had been since they'd existed. And lo and behold, as Conan Doyle's intrepid explorers rounded a clump of bushes...there was a glade full of grazing iguanodons.

Writing this paper, I spent a long time trying to capture that girl's response. You all know the cliché for it; it's the hoariest line in sf. It was my first experience with "sensawunda," of course. But let me do another quick academic detour here to tell you that "sense of wonder" has a long and lofty pedigree, which theorist Stephen Greenblatt kindly assembled for me. According to Greenblatt, Ancient Greek Aristotelian philosophers saw wonder and pleasure as the end—the goal—of poetry. By the Renaissance, an influential Italian critic thought that no one who failed to "excel at arousing wonder" could be called a poet. Thomas Aquinas's teacher hit the nail closest of all. Wonder, he said, was not only intellectual, it was visceral. It caused "a systole of the heart" (79-81).

Despite its hoariness, that, I think, is a hallmark pleasure of the sf text; and although such experiences are rare as a phoenix, it's one I have never lost. When I found the sea vane in Nicola Griffith's *Ammonite* (326), there it was, just as on Conan Doyle's South American plateau: the pause, the stoppage, the visceral clutch. The systole of the heart.

Now grow the explorer up: an English graduate of the late '60s, rather idealistic about politics, rather cynical about art. Dutifully plowing through Barth and Pynchon and Burroughs in the library, buying *Dune* and

Lord of the Rings and slipping off to rock concerts on the side. Then she walks into her local bookshop—about 900 miles from campus—and finds a Victor Gollancz hardback with the old yellow dust-jacket that signals, sf.

This is a fairly literate reader; besides Spenser and Chaucer she has studied the *Aeneid* and known the *Iliad* almost as long as Conan Doyle, and she has a '60s taste for myth. But with her persistent "low" tastes, that yellow cover is a magnet. So she picks it up, reads the title—*The Einstein Intersection*, by some writer she doesn't know—flips it open, and here's Lobey fighting his mutant Minotaur. This time it's not just a systole of the heart; it's, "Wow, they never told me sf writers did stuff like this!"

Mostly, they don't. One of the drawbacks of an old-fashioned humanist tertiary education is that it leaves this awful awareness of style: you can take the girl out of humanism, but you can't take humanism out of the girl. But when an sf writer is a stylist, reading does things for a humanist-educated reader that no realist text can match. It affords—to use another old phrase—an aesthetic pleasure in the text.

Now picture your explorer as a secretary in an outback Queensland town: three or four hundred people, streets wide enough to turn a wool wagon. And three blocks from Main Street, these long, long horizons where a hill goes for two and three miles, nothing but grass and glare. Nothing much in town, either; and only the news agency sells books. She wanders in one day in 1975, and here's a cover that says sf and a name she first saw in a second-hand bin in the Athens Plaka. Ursula K. Le Guin: *The Dispossessed*. So she buys it and takes it home, and ninety or so pages in, Shevek sits down on a park bench with a woman at the other end. She's old and oddly dressed and, "The light was dying fast but she never looked up. She went on reading the proof-sheets of *The Social Organism*" (Le Guin, 90).

The double-take that it's a statue is a given. In those ninety pages, Odo's founding role for Anarres, incidents in Odo's life, and the pronoun "she" crop up often enough: it's not as if you don't know who *she* is. But I still remember getting halfway down the page—stopping, staring at the fan, which was burning its blades off as usual—going back to re-read, and thinking, "Ye Gods—Odo's a *woman* philosopher!"

To you in the United States, of course, this is almost a time warp. Nineteen seventy-five: feminists were re-writing every academic discipline from linguistics to anthropology, feminist utopias were popping out like peas—*Woman on the Edge of Time*, "Houston, Houston, Do You Read?," *The Female Man*. Women's studies were getting off the ground; women were infiltrating every profession. It happened in Australia too. I just wasn't where it happened. I was a proto-feminist—I self-raised my consciousness about 1972, defining the problem with Betty Friedan and transiting the rage phase with Germaine Greer. But I did it in the bush, and for all I knew, I was the only female in Queensland with such weird ideas.

More to the point, the feminist writing I had seen was still in Greer and Millett's phase: mapping women's oppression, triggering women's rage. I had never seen anyone look past that sorry material reality and try to put something in its place. I had never experienced the pleasure of the feminist or feminist-oriented sf text. So it was more than wonder that I felt at this amazing new world, more than aesthetic pleasure; it was a politicized joy, an exciting, empowering glimpse of what women might be. If somebody had told me Isaac Newton was a cross-dressing female scientist, I would have been less galvanized.

Now find your explorer back on the academic treadmill, in a small English Department, where she has worked happily part-time for four or five years; until post-grad students proliferate, and funds shrink, and there is a subtle message that says, "Don't you think you should do a PhD?" So, in a fit of perversity, in this very orthodox Australian department, she says, "OK, I'll do feminism and science fiction," thinking, "Ha, they'll have fits." And to her eternal chagrin, they carol, "Fine, fine."

Well, it could be worse. Many of my students thought I had the most amazing PhD topic ever. When I said, "I'm doing feminism and popular fiction," their eyes would bulge. "You're studying Stephen KING? You're researching sf?" So, even while stepping on the treadmill, I was doing what the French, according to theorist Michel De Certeau, describe as *perruque*: your own work on the company's time (25-28). To top it off, I could indulge what you might call an academic pleasure in the text.

That concept needs another quick preliminary detour through the theory of how texts—meaning literature—are produced. First comes the good old humanist story: the text is the writer's creation, handed down like Moses' tablets, full of universal truths straight from his original mind. Then come the post-humanist theories that lose the writer altogether. Of these, I like best Pierre Macherey's Marxist version, according to which writing is production, using cultural and literary raw materials, a sort of assembly line that pops the text out for readers to consume (66-68). But for an academic, there's another step. Seduced by a text that excites, baffles, or actually infuriates, the academic wants to re-produce: to read that text—which is to say, to re-make it in academic discourse. Then this "product" goes into the academic shark-pond and in its turn competes for printing space, to win its writer what another theorist, Pierre Bourdieu, calls symbolic capital: chiefly, reputation and respect (Johnson, 7).

All of that still lies far ahead when, a lot of sweat, tears, blood, and metamorphoses later, your intrepid explorer finds herself writing a chapter that includes a reading of *The Dispossessed*. And to convey the impact of this feminist utopia, this sf, "Snap!," she describes it in first person, a little more formally than I am doing here. Whereupon her Supervisor comments, "This is an awkward shift in tone."

This anecdote exemplifies what happens when the academic and feminist-sf reader's priorities collide. How do you convey that politicized, feminist, yet integrally science-fictional sense of wonder in a discourse that has been evolved to steamroller out the personal? Without operating from a basic feminist premise, how do you do a feminist reading at all? How, in a word, do you trans-mute the pleasures of *perruque* into company work?

First, there is the problem of how any academic discourse can handle sf. I know that at least one writer-critic whose work I respect greatly considers it impossible, because to him sf isn't literature (Delany, "Science Fiction"). But then, how do you define sf? There's no easy answer that I know, except the one proposed by that same person: it's whatever is marked as sf on the bookshop shelf (Delany, "Gestation," 65). But then, what about someone like Marge Piercy, who marketed *He, She, It* as "literature"? And if sf isn't literature, what, given the lack of a consensus on its actual nature, distinguishes it from other popular forms?

After that tangle comes the question of approach. In the good old humanist days, academic heretics who really wanted their sf *perruque* had to join people like Brian Aldiss and Sam Moskowitz, climbing the ghetto walls, trying to prove that sf was aesthetically O.K., that it actually was "literature." Post-humanist studies have eased this pressure. With Marxist, psychoanalytic, post-colonial, deconstructive, queer, and feminist theorie(s), you may miss the genre's specificity, but the same criteria apply on every bookshop shelf. Every work on there, from Tolstoy's to E.E. (Doc) Smith's, is analyzed and valued in exactly the same way. They are all "texts." And to give only one example, I've found that post-colonial theory, with its foregrounding of colonial discourses, is a very enlightening approach to sf.

As you probably know already, most of these theories have to be retrofitted—to lift another sf word—for feminist use. The feminist theorist has to do what De Certeau argues all consumers of culture do: chop up, twist, retool; or, to use his word, they poach (31). Academics have characterized *Star Trek* fanzines as a classic example of poaching. Like the fanzines, many feminist academics, often under other feminists' reproaches, poach from—chop, twist, put a feminist spin on—post-humanist theory. So doing sf criticism, I had to double-poach: retrofit non-feminist theory while poaching from the pool of non-canonical texts.

How do you poach for a feminist PhD? An answer on a utopian scale would be, dismantle the system that demands PhDs. One on a more modest scale would be, remodel the discourse: include, for example, fictocriticism, or stories, or poems, or rhapsodic passages like those of Hélène Cixous or Susan Griffin. For "high" texts that your readers already know, or can easily access, this often works well. But when you throw Faster Than Light Travel, alternate universes, or a world of androgynes at non-sf readers (which covers most academics, including feminists), and then toss a so-called experimental style on top…

My solution was to dislocate. Most of my PhD dissertation, or thesis, as we say in Australia and the UK, is written in orthodox, impersonal acaspeak. But every now and then, an intervention, to use that hallowed feminist word, comes along to make the genre—and I use the word deliberately, since academia tends to naturalize its work as transparently beyond genre classifications—visible. My interventions use non-academic, often traditional "women's" forms: a poem, a dialogue, but also a computer program and a piece of women's magazine fiction. They drag in the personal. They highlight academic biases. They refuse to let the reader forget that what s/he is reading is no more natural than magazine fiction, and just as partially blind.

Glitches do remain. Samuel Delany once commented that academic sf critics are unclear about both audience and purpose (Samuelson, 33). To adapt David Samuelson's response, much of this stems from "our" links with "our" primary audience (33): trying, for example, to write a PhD dissertation/thesis for three examiners, one of whom—if I was lucky—would know sf, but none of whom would be an expert in sf, horror fiction, *and* Female Romance. To dodge this glitch, traditional literary departments have a tendency to push students toward "high" literature, which lies within most of its members' field of expertise, thus perpetuating the loop.

The bind doubles when you work as a feminist. The consensus of those who know both sides is that in Australia feminism is stronger politically and weaker academically than in the US. In my department, however, there is a glass ceiling for women, let alone avowed feminists. My whole University has only a part-time women's Research Centre. We have no Women's Studies department proper. But even if we did, Women's Studies academics, like many feminists in the '70s, tend to consider sf a genre for men.

So a major headache for the heretic sf postgrad/graduate student, compounded for the feminist, is finding a supervisor well-versed enough to get the project off the ground. My best chance was a male specialist in popular fiction who is strongly sympathetic to feminism. As Justine and Helen and I once decided, for a graduate/postgrad student in Australia, having an sf-specialist supervisor would get you trashed for unfair advantage, and first-person stories suggest it is not always better in the US. My Supervisor did wonders. But I will never forget how, two chapters into the sf section of my thesis, he moved to a southern job, and I gave him a Farside farewell card and wrote on it, *I can do EVA without a hand-line, but do I have to fix the Hubble while I'm out?* He read it and asked, "What's EVA?"

What we have here is actually the loneliness of the long-distance PhD student. Helen and Justine re-marked on the problem, doing sf in English or History Departments. But at a Women's Studies conference I spoke to someone writing a thesis on feminist dis-course, and in the heartland of Australian feminist academia, I learned that she also felt isolated. For the actual work, though, it is more than lonely; it can be dangerous. Living in North Queensland, outside the sf community, doing a PhD in the literary equivalent of freefall, was sometimes very near a God trip. The texts propose, you dispose; no other critical voices in-tervene, and the texts can't fight back.

Again, the feminist dimension deepens supervi-sion glitches. Though my Supervisor did not know the primary texts, he turned my academic chapters into subway graffiti; but he would not comment on the interventions at all. In the course of supervising my six-year part-time thesis, he reached the position taken by many male academics; not wholly, I feel, through sexism or lack of interest: that is, to bow out of what Australian indigenes call "women's business" in fear that if they venture in, they'll get thumped.

This political crux also left me as something of a third person peculiar at least once. As Sandra Harding powerfully argues, if white middle-class feminists claim they have learnt from the standpoint of black, lesbian, Chicana, and Third-World feminists, how are we to deny men can do the same (145)? In my work on male and female sf writers, I found at least one male sf writer, John Varley, who uses feminist discourse to produce women characters that still don't get up my now highly sensitized feminist nose. But when I remarked that by all the feminist-established criteria Varley's *Titan* was a lesbian text, my male Supervisor went ballistic, saying, in effect, that in claiming a man could write a lesbian text, his female student wasn't being "feminist."

This topsy-turvy incident highlights another crux. It's difficult enough having to define sf for the academic project, but how do you define *feminist* sf?

This, it seems, is the sixty-four thousand-answer question. Critics are the first academic resort. Some offer the equivalent of what Katie King calls "taxonomies of feminism" (124). Others classify the same texts as feminist sf or feminist utopias (Roberts, 86-111), writers are included in one list and omitted from another, and you find hierarchies that put "feminist" above "women's" sf (Lefanu, 87-93). As Justine and Helen and I once discussed, academic feminists can ignore—or simply remain ignorant of—anything not published by the Women's Press, or just, to poach Evelyn Fox Keller's title for the biography of Barbara McClintock, not have "a feeling for the organism."

I hear you saying, there is another choice. Get out of free fall: go to the sf community. Check out the zines and look at letters and interviews from writers understood—by you or somebody else—to be feminist. Or contact them directly, through something like the Fem-SF listserv, and ask, "Do you consider your-self a feminist? Whose work, including yours, do you consider feminist sf?"

But in the sf community, you find more answers than the critics gave. The Internet has a whole site devoted to definitions of feminism. A recent listserv discussion of what feminist sf is came nowhere near achieving consensus. But for a third person peculiar, entering any sf community raises questions as difficult as those in academia.

Mostly, these center round the interaction of criticism and personal acquaintance. I'll begin with a male member of the sf community whose networking helped put me here. He gave me contacts, discussed texts and ideas on email, lent me books, read my work. A good way into the friendship, I sent him a piece on a novel I greatly admire, Connie Willis's *Lincoln's Dreams*. After some eight pages' rhapsody about its innovations, its structure, its brilliant narrative techniques, I suddenly remembered I was a post-humanist feminist. And when I looked at Willis's text through Annette Kolodny's lenses of race and gender, I found an alarming absence of black characters or voices in a novel supposedly about the American Civil War.

So, fairly embarrassed at my lapse, I clapped a critique on the essay's tail and sent it off to my mate. I got back a note saying, in effect, a lot of American readers are going to get upset at some Australian lecturing them on race problems, and a warning that, in fandom, I might have started an international incident.

This was somewhat startling, but it could have been an individual response. I had great hopes of discovering if this was so when I was accepted into the Fem-SF listserv discussion group. An sf community at last! A woman's community, and a feminist one at that! Now I was really at the Galactic heart.

After a while, though, I noticed an implicit hierarchy, which someone else also remarked on: nobody said so, but there seemed to be gatekeepers. If you were new, you could make a posting, but a gatekeeper might well challenge you; if you survived, your posting was mostly ignored. In time I was reminded of the poem about the Boston Cabots, who spoke only to Lowells, and the Lowells, who spoke only to God. In this case, the Cabots were a personally acquainted or long-term group of sf community members, and the Lowells were established feminist sf writers. The hopeful sf readers/academics—and I don't speak only of myself—were certainly not God.

What startled the third person peculiar a good deal more was how little this feminist sf community seemed aware of what I, from my North Australian crow-perch, understood as the issues and history of feminism. Reading the famous *Khatru* symposium, I found Suzy McKee Charnas in 1974-5 expounding what in 1980 the academic feminists would name standpoint theory (Smith, 13). I found Joanna Russ and Luise White working through the still vexed question of women's killing fantasies (72-79). I found James Tiptree posing questions about why we mother that still go unanswered (20-21). Shortly before, I had read a 1990 interview with Karen Joy Fowler, Lisa Goldstein, and Pat Murphy about "The State of Feminism in SF." Though Goldstein et al. were explicitly called feminist sf writers (Counsil, 21), and they knew sf backwards, they hardly seemed aware of second-wave history like the sex-wars—probably the most crucial single happening in '80s feminism—let alone separatism or Goddess worship. To me, these are not merely academic matters. Theories of pornography or political lesbianism were not developed behind academic desks but through interactions in the home, the workplace, the street. They were finessed into libraries afterwards; but they feed straight back into personal politics: do I write to the papers about that poster, do I join Reclaim the Night marches, do I give evidence to the Meese commission? Do I join a separatist commune, do I change my doctor because he's a man? These issues are still both academic hot-points and cruces of everyday feminist life. Yet Goldstein et al. left all this unmentioned. It seemed as if these writers, as Karen Joy Fowler remarked in a postscript to *Khatru*—had "lost their [feminist] edge" (Smith, 129).

In the same way, many of the Fem-SF listserv participants in a '96 discussion of feminism seemed unaware they were doing things, such as recounting undifferentiated "women's" experience, that feminist theorists—from white women getting their knuckles rapped by black women to straight women being called by lesbians—learnt to avoid quite a while ago. I was startled by this: because most of these people came from the US, where feminist coffee-shops, feminist book-stores, separatist communes, Wiccan festivals—the whole breadth of gynocentric feminist culture—was supposed to be a twenty-year-old reality. I had only read about it. What was more, I considered my knowledge out-of-date, because according to Katie King's description of the speed of feminist thinking (71), what came out of printed books was already four and five years down the wave.

So it astonished me to come on a reverse time-warp, so to speak, when as a third person peculiar I was ready to disparage the academic ignorance of sf. More worrying, to my academic side, were posts defending Marion Zimmer Bradley as a feminist writer, not on the basis of her texts' content, but because of her health problems, personal problems, and her well-doing to others. Now, I may have been seduced by the post-humanist reduction of writers to author-functions, and perhaps I have internalized masculinist academic criteria for excellence. I have made a ground-tenet, like so many others, of the value of women's experience. As a feminist, I would be delighted to argue that Bradley's texts draw power and passion and even "truth" from personal experience. But as an academic, I grow extremely worried when someone tells me, in effect, "Don't say what you honestly think of this work, because of what you know about the writer's life." This suggests to me that my male friend is NOT an aberration in sf communities. And moreover, that if I want to keep my academic integrity, I must stay outside the (feminist) sf community, or I will be expected to put the personal before the political in ways that I, personally, can't accept.

I feel this opens a major question for the sf/academic interface and, indeed, for feminist practice as a whole, which has long struggled with the question of criticism. I've repeatedly been told that the personal/communal element is specific to sf. But how do you enter an sf community and retain academic honesty about the texts? How do feminists combine the personal and the critical without being viewed as either Pollyanna or the Wicked Witch?

Obviously, these questions intersect my concerns as an academic approaching an sf community, but I think they are also crucial for feminists in general. I have no overall solution. I have found a gathering consensus in (published) feminist thinking that goes past Yes/No answers to insist on tensions, tight-rope walking, and contradictions acknowledged—to use Teresa de Lauretis' phrase—but not resolved (144). About 1985, Linda Gordon addressed this in terms of writing women's history. Speaking from debates on the value of experience, the myth of objectivity, the choice between chronicling what women have suffered and praising what they've done, she wrote: "There may be no objective canons of historiography, but there are better and worse pieces of history. The challenge is precisely to maintain this tension between accuracy and mythic power" (22).

To me, writing a feminist PhD that included sf, the question of maintaining tension between the mythic and the accurate, the personal and the critical, was anything but academic. In my own practice, it might mean including the writer's personal dimension while skirting the biography trap; critiquing without animosity, but also without compromise; putting "myself" in the text, without over-privileging "women's experience." In general, I found myself repeating what so many women have been saying since the '80s began: maybe we have to raise our boiling points, to avoid the horrendous previous personal schisms, and work to keep our feminism as a hard-won personal praxis/ principle, while forming coalitions with others who are not—are not and never will be—Us. The conflicts at the UN World Conference on Women, at Beijing in 1995, indicate how hard this still is.

And perhaps we have to change our thinking even more radically. I saw sf communit(ies) as offering both the sort of in-house knowledge I academically needed, and the sort of personal contact and support we all desire. Maybe I should have remembered Martin and Mohanty's well-known academic essay called, "What's Home Got To Do With It?" They take up the memoirs of another feminist historian, Minnie Bruce Pratt, who found that every home is an illusion, created by exclusion and Othering, never existing for long, never for real. Maybe, then, my expectations of the sf community were also unreal. I should have remembered that, however much feminists, in particular, long to find some place they can be welcomed and comfortable, that is not, to use Carol Emshwiller's evocative title, "The Start of the End of it All." I should have recalled what Linda Kauffman once said: "I never thought feminism was about happiness. I thought it was about justice" (274). I would like to think that sharing the standpoint of a third person peculiar could make this insight more positive. Could help us to live as if we want a home, but as if any community, even in sf, even in feminism, is not primarily for safety and permanence. As if it is rather a place where we're always opening doors and uprooting furniture; making sure, in effect, that the "home" we build doesn't turn into a trap.

Works Cited

bes shahar, eluki. *Hellflower*. New York: Daw, 1991.

Bourdieu, Pierre. *The Field of Cultural Production: Essays on Art and Literature*. Ed. Randal Johnson. Oxford: Polity, 1993.

Charnas, Suzy McKee. "No Road." *Women of Vision*. Ed. Denise Du Pont. New York: St. Martin's, 1988. 143-62.

Counsil, Wendy. "The State of Feminism In Science Fiction: An Interview with Karen Joy Fowler, Lisa Goldstein and Pat Murphy." *Science Fiction Eye* August (1990): 21-31.

De Certeau, Michel. *The Practice of Everyday Life*. Trans. Steven F. Rendall. Berkeley: University of California Press, 1984.

De Lauretis, Teresa. "Eccentric Subjects: Feminist Theory and Historical Consciousness." *Feminist Studies* 16.1 (1990): 115-50.

Delany, Samuel R. *The Einstein Intersection*. 1967. London: Victor Gollancz, 1968.

——. "The Gestation of Genres: Literature, Fiction, Romance, Science Fiction, Fantasy…" *Intersections: Fantasy and Science Fiction*. Eds. George E. Slusser and Eric S. Rabkin. Carbondale: University of Southern Illinois Press, 1987. 63-73.

——. "Science Fiction and 'Literature'—Or, The Conscience of the King." *Starboard Wine: More Notes on the Language of Science Fiction*. New York: Dragon, 1984. 81-100.

Gordon, Linda. "What's New in Women's History." *Feminist Studies/Critical Studies*. Ed. Teresa de Lauretis. Houndmills: Macmillan, 1988. 20-30.

Greenblatt, Stephen J. *Marvelous Possessions: The Wonder of the New World*. Oxford: Clarendon, 1991.

Griffith, Nicola. *Ammonite*. London: HarperCollins, 1993.

Harding, Sandra. "Reinventing Ourselves as Other: More New Agents of History and Knowledge." *American Feminist Thought at Century's End: A Reader*. Ed. Linda S. Kauffman. Cambridge MA, Oxford UK: Blackwell, 1993. 140-64.

Johnson, Randal. "Editor's Introduction." Pierre Bourdieu. *The Field of Cultural Production: Essays on Art and Literature*. Ed. Randal Johnson. Oxford: Polity, 1993. 1-25.

Kauffman, Linda S. "The Long Goodbye: Against Personal Testimony, or An Infant Grifter Grows Up." *American Feminist Thought at Century's End: A Reader*. Ed. Linda S. Kauffman. Cambridge, MA, Oxford UK: Blackwell, 1993. 258-77.

King, Katie. *Theory in its Feminist Travels: Conversations in U.S. Women's Movements*. Bloomington: Indiana University Press, 1994.

Le Guin, Ursula K. *The Dispossessed*. 1974. St. Albans: Panther, 1975.

Lefanu, Sarah. *In the Chinks of the World Machine: Feminism and Science Fiction*. London: Women's Press, 1988.

Macherey, Pierre. *A Theory of Literary Production*. 1978. Trans. Geoffrey Wall. London: Routledge and Kegan Paul, 1986.

Martin, Biddy and Chandra Mohanty. "What's Home Got to Do with It?" *Feminist Studies, Critical Studies*. Ed. Teresa de Lauretis. Bloomington: Indiana University Press, 1986. 191-212.

Roberts, Robin. *A New Species: Gender and Science in Science Fiction*. Urbana: University of Illinois Press, 1993.

Samuelson, David N. "Necessary Constraints: Samuel R. Delany on Science Fiction." *Foundation* 60 (1994): 211-41.

Smith, Jeffrey D. *Khatru: Symposium: Women in Science Fiction*. 1975. Madison: Corflu No. 10, 1993.

Tales of Earth:
Terraforming in Recent Women's SF

Donna Haraway once described sf as a place where "possible worlds are constantly reinvented in the contest for very real, present worlds" (5). World-building is indeed an identifying feature of both sf and fantasy, its importance acknowledged by the presence of d.i.y. manuals (Le Guin, "Do-It-Yourself," 121), its pleasures shared by writers and readers both. At base, most sf and fantasy worlds have a common feature: they are habitable by humans. But if sf worlds are not directly compatible, then there is a further option: either humans are altered to suit the world, or the world is tailored to fit humanity. This concept of remodeling a planet's atmosphere and/or biosphere is known as terraforming.

The *Encyclopedia of Science Fiction* dates the term from Jack Williamson's coinage in 1951, but traces the concept from Olaf Stapledon's *Last and First Men* in 1930 (Clute and Nicholls, 1213). The date is not insignificant. Andrew Ross, among others, has discussed the between-wars "cults of science and technological invention that embellished a positivist religion" shared by right and left alike, with an "unstinting faith in the progressive virtues of science" (105). Its brief but vaulting high noon of credence in human capability is memorialized in William Gibson's "The Gernsback Continuum" (1981). To such an age, remodeling a planet might appear just one more ambitious project to contemplate along with stellar travel and viable nuclear energy.

At the same time, such a concept springs straight from the cultural matrix of science fiction: it is a genre founded in and on the period, the ideologies, and the discourses of colonial capitalism. They supply sf's founding narratives of exploration, first contact, space wars, and the framework of planetary expansion, imperial power-structures, and colonial settlement. From colonialism comes also that fundamental sf binary of Human/Alien, the analogue of the Colonizer/Colonized pair, with its spectrum of ideological and emotional baggage traced by post-colonial theorists like Homi Bhabha (18-36), from passionate and exotic desire to self-recognition, to paranoid xenophobia.

Colonial capitalism also supplies the economic concepts of expansion, exploitation, and annexation of natural resources beyond a culture's geographic boundaries. More to the point, nineteenth century colonial expansion produced the ideologies that justify this attitude — that make it *all right* for a nation or culture to appropriate land and resources, yea, at times, even *necessary*, if not—to use that latest imperial shibboleth—*indispensable* (Neilsen, 5). And from that view springs the still-enduring and yet more pernicious assumption that it is all right because there will always be more *somewhere*. It began, perhaps, when Columbus christened the Indies a New World; it funds imaginative as well as economic resources, even for canonical writers like Dickens and Bronte, who can shunt unwanted characters off to Australia, or find cursed colonial treasure—including women—in the Caribbean. And this presumption of limitless Elsewheres underlies the imaginative economy of sf, which functions, as Haraway says, on an endless supply of reinvented possible worlds.

This particular cultural matrix is also intrinsically Western, as fundamentally white and, as has now been pointed out almost ad nauseam, alarmingly masculinist. Such critiques have, with equal justice, been made about Western science, which is not merely an analogue of colonial capitalism but deeply and inextricably interwoven with it, from its discourses and its goals to the funding on which it operates. Both are part of what may be called a hegemonic worldview, a worldview operating as well, if not better, in the twentieth century of postindustrial, megacorporate, decolonized but global capitalism as it did in the colonial nineteenth century. The assumption of more to be had, of resources for the taking and room needing only to be made, has also continued in sf. It is evident in the *Encyclopedia*'s history of terraforming. Named and developed in the 1950s, becoming "common-place in the '60s and '70s (Clute and Nicholls, 1215), it is alive and overwhelmingly healthy in the 1990s with Kim Stanley Robinson's award-winning Mars trilogy. The *Encyclopedia*'s entry takes for granted that such a feat of meticulously grounded imagination—what David Brin calls engineering sf, meaning the solution of concrete if "unreal" problems (11-12)—is ethically and ideologically acceptable.

Growing more familiar, nowadays, is an opposing view summed up, ironically, by an entry from a Microsoft encyclopedia CD—sponsored by the world's current richest capitalist:

> No population, human or otherwise, can grow indefinitely; eventually, some biotic or abiotic variable will begin to limit population growth. (Zimmerman, 1)

Also ironically, this resistant strain was engendered by the same technological advances and cultural change as colonial capitalism. It took seed with the English Romantics in the early nineteenth century and grew with the equally powerful influence of American transcendentalists like Emerson and, above all, Thoreau. Both schools figured in a fundamental shift in the relation of humans to Nature. The new relationship is described by Haraway as a form of "salvation history" (9): the industrial West, which itself reduced Nature from menacing opponent to dwindling resource, now re-instates Nature as an Eden which, if but regained, would salve all our civilized woes. The vision was first articulated by Wordsworth, turning from the urban political squalor of the later French Revolution to the vision of Nature as moral nurse in "Tintern Abbey" (ll.107-111). Gaining force with Thoreau's vision of life in the wilderness, the view widened into the first environmental movement, resulting in legislation to create national parks, forests, and wildlife systems, implemented in the early 1900s by Theodore Roosevelt

(Zimmerman, 2-3). The US, which seems the heartland of industrial capitalism, thus appears to be the historical leader of its counterforce.

Environmental protection reappeared with Franklin Roosevelt in the 1930s, but we know it best in the '60s and '70s, in the wake of Rachel Carson's famous *Silent Spring* (1962). In the early 1970s, with 20 million Americans celebrating Earth Day, the current Green Movement began. After the powerful political innovations of the '70s, in the wake of a somnolent '80s and the abortive Earth Summit in 1992 (Zimmerman, 3-6), the Green Movement now appears to be an analogue of feminism: a cause whose goals remain imperatively unachieved but whose fervor is just slightly passé.

Reinventing possible worlds, sf has paralleled this contest for the real earth with a resistant strain of world-building. As a '60s adolescent, I had my sense of Nature remodeled most powerfully, on the one hand, by Tolkien's *Lord of the Rings*, and on the other, by Frank Herbert's *Dune* (1965). If Tolkien made me see the preciousness of trees, Herbert showed me the whole forest. Not a small part of my pleasure in *Dune* had nothing to do with ramping sand-worms, glamorized Bedouin, and recycled *jihads*: it came from seeing an entire planet as an exquisitely balanced but absolutely fragile ecological whole.

In *Dune*, however, ecological awareness does not expand into critique of, let alone resistance to colonial appropriation. It never occurs to Herbert or his heroes to leave the planet *alone*. But in the '70s, the historical Green Movement joined what Tom Moylan calls a bloc of "autonomous oppositional movements" that "challeng[e] corporate and allied state interests" and are "deeply infused with the politics of autonomy, democratic socialism, ecology, and especially feminism" (11). On the critical/theoretical side, the combined approaches of feminism and post-colonialism, in particular, have produced ever deeper and more searching deconstructions of the capitalist-colonialist nexus, including its colleague/accomplice, science.

Such streams of critique emerged in the later '70s, when feminism was infiltrating academic disciplines from literature to anthropology, with texts from Elaine Showalter's *A Literature of Their Own,* to Sally Slocum's "Woman the Gatherer: Male Bias in Anthropology" (1975.) In 1980 Carolyn Merchant pioneered feminist deconstructions of Nature as seen in the scientific/capitalist worldview. As post-colonial founding figures such as Edward Said and Chinua Achebe foregrounded the Western construction of Others in *Orientalism* or found racism in canonical writers like Conrad, feminist literary critics began to deconstruct the equally masculinist colonial discourse of such writers. In the '80s, Rebecca Stott outlined the construction of nature as a feminine body in Rider Haggard's Africa, while Gail Ching-Liang Low explored the marginalizing of women that produced a male homosocial community among his black and white men (110). Bette London read Africa in *Heart of Darkness* as the ultimate colonial Other: black, feminine, and terrifying (237). Meanwhile, Evelyn Fox Keller and Ruth Bleier, among others, interrogated the masculinist biases of science, biases tied insolubly to colonial capitalism by the "eroticized and gendered trope[s]" as Haraway puts it (205), of exploration and colonization, envisaged upon a nature/ Earth read as passive bodies, unveiled/penetrated/used by virile explorers/scientists/capitalists. And as Anne Mellor shows, these tropes are there from the beginning of sf, flourishing, naked if not unquestioned, in Mary Shelley's *Frankenstein* (226-28).

The vital presence of feminism in this interrogative coalition is also evident in sf; part of its consequence is the foregrounding in opposition of women sf writers, a trend evident far earlier than in theory. It appears overtly and ferociously in Ursula Le Guin's 1968 "preachment," as she called it, *The Word for World is Forest* (Introduction, *Word*, 152). There visions of colonial rape and despoliation issue in a final battle, deaths, and expulsion of the colonists, portraits of indubitably white Western men who easily double for American soldiers in Vietnam. *Word* remodels the staple narrative of colonial settlement and expansion as a violent denunciation, contesting the real world, not by inventing a new one so much as by comprehensively indicting the old.

Feminism is powerfully evident when the entire colonial frame of settlement and human expansion is not merely critiqued but demolished by Joanna Russ's 1977 novel *We Who Are About To*... All the shipwrecked passengers, neither strong-minded explorers nor worthy colonists, eventually die. And with them goes Wordsworth's golden image of Nature as nurturing and friendly to humans:

> Think of Earth. Kind old home. Think
> of the Arctic. Of Labrador. Of Southern
> India in June. Think of smallpox and

> plague and earthquake and ringworm…
> Think…of tsunamis, liver fluke, the
> Asian brown bear. Kind old home.…
> The darling place.
>
> Think of Death Valley…in August. (20)

Le Guin would offer a more radical but less negative re-vision in 1973, with "Vaster than Empires and More Slow." Rather than adjusting settlers to suit it, this world eats—psychically and perhaps physically absorbs—a member of the exploring expedition. The character of the casualty, an outcast with paranormal powers, makes this story an interesting contrast to Isaac Asimov's "Sucker Bait" (1954). There another outcast, a human database, saves the exploring team from fatal contact with a beautiful but secretly lethal planet. But where Asimov's explorers recoil on a note of suppressed hysteria—one might almost say xenophobia—Le Guin's leave a world quieted by union with an Other who has been willingly assimilated. There is a new and entirely paradoxical irony in their lost crewman's memorial: "Sensor Osden, left as a colonist" ("Vaster," 199).

Such resistant world-building is not always successful, although it seems to operate better among writers who, however covertly, espouse some form of feminism. Lip service is paid to nature in Marion Zimmer Bradley's *Darkover Landfall* (1972), a novel more notorious for the storm over its very non-feminist attitudes to abortion. Her ship-wrecked colonists quickly forget respect for the chance-acquired planet in the need to possess "our world" (88), and the narrative remains firmly enmeshed in the storyline of colonial settlement. Nor is there any suggestion of a contesting native life. Darkover has been a planet where Bradley herself could contest, explore, and re-write issues of gender, and then offer other women writers "a safe space in which to try creativity" (Introduction, *Keeper's*, 12). Nevertheless, the fundamentally colonial nature of the setting and narrative and the right of humans to be on Darkover are never queried.

The historic specificity of such contests appears with Le Guin's 1978 novella, *The Eye of the Heron*. Here questions of violence and pacifism, again formulated in gendered and explicitly feminist terms, are worked out on a magnificent, human-compatible planet conveniently empty of sentient inhabitants. In the late '60s Le Guin was concerned with the common oppositional causes of sexism, racism, and the Vietnam war: by 1978 she had focused on more straitly feminist issues. As a result, a text interrogating traditional gender patterns speaks with the new voice of essential feminism about "men" and "women":

> "[S]ometimes…[men] are so stupid,
> so stuffed with theories… They go in
> straight lines only, and won't stop.…
> It seems to me that where men are
> weak and dangerous is in their vanity. A
> woman…is a centre. But a man isn't, he's
> a reaching out." (Le Guin, *Heron,* 169)

But the same text takes for granted the fundamental colonial doctrine of *terra nullius*, the "empty" Other earth. And with it, leaves unquestioned the basic colonial solution when the pacifists go into separate exile:

if we can't fix the problem here, we can always take it somewhere else.

This fresh start assumption operates even more disconcertingly in Nicola Griffith's award-winning 1993 novel *Ammonite*. Its construction of a world that a male-specific virus has barred to men, its hypothesis of parthenogenic birth, and its powerful myths of women's self-discovery and self-constructed wholeness are, from a feminist or even queer point of view, wholly admirable. There is a strong strand of anti-capitalism in the final awareness that the women of Jeep will have their Utopia only till the Company finds a virus cure. Yet a woman of Jeep, and of the more idyllic farming community at that, is shown trapping and starving to death a local life-form, just to get its undamaged hide (315-18). That this victim is clearly male as well as sentient suggests a collision rather than intersection between the competing causes of feminism—perhaps essentialist, and clearly overtly lesbian—and post-colonialism. Even though it is explicitly condemned in the novel, it may be read as a symbolic statement of men's superfluity or tragic irrelevance. But it is also exemplary colonial exploitation of a luckless native, erased as just another beast.

Again, open attempts to attack capitalism as that now familiar ogre, The Company, may not escape the colonial nets of the reinvented possible world. In Sheri Tepper's *The Enigma Score* (1987), a villainous Company plots to declare native life forms insentient, freeing it to exploit the planet, but is foiled by an alliance of natives and "good," also exploited, human colonists. In *Raising the Stones* (1991), a decolonized sensibility appears in the portrait of a System—solar and political—with a protective, if somewhat futile "Native Authority." Again, native life-forms defeat colonial villains and save "good" colonists. This time *terra nullius* gets a new twist, for the presiding alien on Hobbs Land is a "god that really work[s]." (What, Tepper asks in an interview, if "people had a god that really worked?" [*Locus*, 69]). This is a protective divinity that lives in symbiosis with its colonists, literally terraforming the landscape in the image each succeeding life-form provides. Yet in both novels, binaries of Self/Other, Colonizer/Colonized align with the sf division of Human/Alien: colonizers are human, however diverse, good or bad; natives are not-human and are divided into further classic binaries of good/beautiful/powerful and ugly/powerful/evil. In *Stones*, the ugly natives are as evil as the human villains. Nor, at any point, does either narrative question the right of the colonists to be where they are.

Nor does a self-reflexive consciousness of post-colonial issues guarantee resistance to colonial tradition. Connie Willis' witty *Uncharted Territory* (1994) mixes gender confusions and clever interrogations of colonial narratives with up-to-date satires on natives who will exploit the future tourists. Yet the novel closes with the female narrator and her explorer partner riding off into the sunset of an Uncharted Territory whose one sense, as a land of hitherto repressed emotion, is matched by that of a yet unexplored world, offered to her as a colonial explorer's ongoing Paradise, a kind of marvelous gift.

Women writers can also reproduce the colonial standpoint unhesitatingly, right up to terraforming that wipes out native species, as the "platytheres" are killed on C.J. Cherryh's planet in *Cyteen* (1989), or the equally unquestioned restructuring of the planetary biosphere in Lois Bujold's *Komarr* (1997*)*, and indeed, on her other two Barrayaran worlds. In these books Cherryh explores alternate sexualities as well as renovates the traditional mother/daughter relationship, while Bujold conducts admirable explorations of gender issues, subversions of masculinist tradition in space opera and the depiction of sf heroes, and remarkable articulations of women's experience. Yet for both writers, terraforming is an unquestioned part of heroic struggles for colonial survival, with no whisper of doubt that the colonists may and can erase an unfriendly ecology for their own benefit.

A contrast to these late '80s and late '90s preservations of orthodoxy is Alison Sinclair's 1996 novel *Blue Heart*. On yet another water world, reminiscent of David Brin's *Startide Rising* (1983) or Joan Slonczewski's *The Door into Ocean* (1986), colonists adapting to the environment, in this case by becoming amphibious, confront the divisive political and ethical question: should colonial occupation proceed until these assimilations are outdated and the whole planet is terraformed to suit land-dwelling humans? Here, for the first time, terraforming is specifically foregrounded as an exploitive process, and the issue proceeds through political debates as well as outright physical battle against capitalism. We are back to the holistic planetary vision of *Dune* and the thoroughly oppositional position of Le Guin in 1968; the change of arena marks the real time shift from the era of Vietnam to that of longdrawn ecological campaigns. Yet even in this novel, although terraforming is finally repudiated, the right of the assimilated humans to remain is neither questioned nor denied.

A more absolute re-vision of the colonial narrative appears in Janet Kagan's *Hellspark* (1988). A graduate of *Star Trek* spin-offs, Kagan offers an updated, decolonized version of Le Guin's "Vaster than Empires"—rather than mapping a *terra nullius*, her hero is a linguistic specialist summoned by signs of skulduggery among scientists who must decide if a planet's native life is sentient. If so, as with the more regulated colonization depicted in Tepper's *Enigma Score*, the exploiters will have to extract their claws. And despite the efforts of the villain, this eventually happens. The planet is declared off-limits for ANY colonization, and all the humans, good or bad, pack their traps and leave.

In Haraway's terms, we have here a complete reversal of industrialized, capitalist humanity's search for redemption in some previously untouched world. Rather than destroy native life, assimilate itself, or fight off its own Dark Halves as the price of admission, humanity is flatly ejected, leaving the now legally franked native life forms to exploit their resources as they choose. But in the real world, to turn back time and leave the colonial Eden undamaged is impossible; Kagan rather produces another wistful compensatory fiction to counter what the Fatal Impact, to use Alan Moorehead's famous title, has done. The political struggle of *Blue Heart*, with its powerful enunciation of ecological respect and its perforce acceptance of established colonizers, is closer to the real world Haraway examines in decolonized Madagascar: there colonial scientists were first ejected altogether, then allowed back strictly on Malagasy terms, to assist in the struggle for protected resources and a sustainable economy (268-75). Such a compromise may be the best the real, apparent post-colonial world can achieve.

But where, you ask, does this paper discuss women writers and terraforming? The answer is: it doesn't. The women writers in this survey just don't use it much. But this does not imply a now familiar *en bloc* claim for female superiority. The organicist view, as Haraway calls it, valorizes women's knowledge as more holist, less hostile to nature, able to offer a "true[er]," more "fully human knowledge" opposed to masculinist or Western science (256). But as Haraway points out, this replicates the oppositional strategy of constructing an ideal Other — women, primates, Asia — with just the properties that the writer's culture lacks and needs or fears and rejects, yet with no awareness of the historical and textual forms of power and violence built into such visions. For Haraway, "living in the 'East' — whether that place is found inside a cell, in the right half of the brain, in the Sacred Hills of Dakota, in mothering before or beyond patriarchy — is no solution for living in the 'West'" (258). So too, this brief survey indicates that women writers have no inbuilt superiority in their grasp of post-colonial issues, up to and including terraforming. Even overt or covert feminism is not proof against recurring colonial certainties. Nor does the chronology suggest an improvement over time. *Word for World* came out in 1968 and *Hellspark* in 1988, but *Cyteen* and *Komarr*, the most unquestioning endorsements of terraforming, appeared in 1989 and 1997. "Progress" in this case seems another Victorian myth.

This stasis parallels events in the real, apparent world, where in 1989 Carolyn Merchant felt qualified hope for "an ecological transformation" (270), but where resistance to political correctness is now turning greenies into tree-huggers. Yet the urgencies of ecological preservation and altered attitudes to the world around us will not disappear in this new millennium. If sf is to remain the genre of the future, it may have to terraform its own assumptions about the worlds it invents. What place is there for colonial settlement narratives and endless off-Earth cornucopias in a real, decolonized world? Where does an sf text look, not at legendary victories over a mythical Company, but at post-Company problems among the native sentients? What sf text deals with tribal factions, beyond-slum lack of food, water, and medical supplies, and battles to balance endangered animals' survival against human need for fuel and arable land? Where, in our slick images of stellar flights and planetary urban sprawls, are the eyes and voices of the once colonized? Is sf, in fact, being left in the colonial past? Is it truly just escapist fiction after all? Perhaps we may have to interrogate, not merely the glorious imperial vision of terraforming, but the entire idea of more elsewhere—or even the entire option of other worlds. Maybe it is time to concede that there is no Elsewhere: that this is all we have. Then sf writers might turn their great resources of ingenuity and imagination into going more boldly where humanity has always been: into imagining a better future for this by no means inexhaustible earth.

Works Cited

Achebe, Chinua. "An Image of Racism in Conrad's *Heart of Darkness." Heart of Darkness*. Ed. Robert Kimbrough, New York: Norton, 1985. 251-61.

Asimov, Isaac. "Sucker Bait." 1954. *The Martian Way*. 1955. London: Panther, 1967. 117-92.

Bhabha, Homi. "The Other Question…." *Screen* 24.6 (1983): 18-36.

Bleier, Ruth. "Introduction." *Feminist Approaches to Science*. New York: Pergamon, 1986. 1-17.

Bradley, Marion Zimmer. *Darkover Landfall*. 1970. London: Arrow, 1978.

——. "Introduction." *The Keeper's Price*. Ed. Marion Zimmer Bradley, New York: Daw, 1980. 7-15.

Brin, David. "Running Out of Speculative Niches: A Crisis for Hard SF?" *Hard Core Science Fiction*. Eds. George E. Slusser and Eric S. Rabkin. Carbondale: University of Southern Illinois, 1986. 8-13.

Bujold, Lois McMaster. *Komarr*. New York: Baen, 1997.

Cherryh, C. J. *Cyteen*. 1988. London: New English Library, 1989.

Ching-Liang Low, Gail. "His Stories? Narratives and Images of Imperialism." *New Formations* 12 (1990): 97-123.

Clute, John, and Peter Nicholls, eds. *The Encyclopedia of Science Fiction*, 2nd ed. London: Orbit, 1993.

Griffith, Nicola. *Ammonite*. London: Grafton, 1993.

Haraway, Donna. *Primate Visions: Gender, Race, and Nature in the World of Modern Science.* London: Verso, 1992.

Kagan, Janet. *Hellspark.* New York: Tor, 1988.

Keller, Evelyn Fox. *Reflections on Gender and Science.* New Haven: Yale University Press, 1985.

Le Guin, Ursula K. "Do-It-Yourself Cosmology," *Parabola II 3* (1977); Reprinted in Susan Wood, *The Language of the Night: Essays on Fantasy and Science Fiction.* New York: Perigee, 1977. 121-25.

——. *The Eye of the Heron,* 1978. *The Eye of the Heron and Other Stories.* Ed. Virginia Kidd. St. Albans: Panther, 1980. 209-51.

——. "Vaster than Empires and More Slow." *The Wind's Twelve Quarters.* 1975. New York: Bantam, 1976. 167-99.

——. Introduction to *The Word for World is Forest,* (British Edition, 1977. Reprinted in Susan Wood, *The Language of the Night: Essays on Fantasy and Science Fiction.* New York: Perigee, 1979.149-54, at 152.

Locus. "Sheri S. Tepper: Aspiring Up." Unattributed Article, 4 (1991): 69.

London, Bette. "Reading Race and Gender in Conrad's Dark Continent." *Criticism,* XXXI.3 (1989): 235-252.

Mellor, Anne K. "Possessing Nature: The Female In *Frankenstein.*" *Romanticism and Feminism.* Ed. Anne K. Mellor. Bloomington: Indiana University Press, 1988. 220-32.

Merchant, Carolyn. *The Death of Nature: Women, Ecology, and the Scientific Revolution.* New York: Harper and Row. 1980.

Moylan, Tom. *Demand The Impossible: Science Fiction and the Utopian Imagination*, New York: Methuen, 1986.

Neilson, Heather. "Big Words: Issues in American Self-Representation." *The Australasian Journal of American Studies,* 17.1 (1998): 3-21.

Ross, Andrew. *Strange Weather: Culture, Science and Technology in the Age of Limits.* London: Verso, 1991.

Russ, Joann. *We Who Are About To....* 1977. London: Women's Press, 1987.

Said, Edward W. *Orientalism.* 1978. Harmondsworth: Penguin Books, 1985.

Sinclair, Alison. *Blueheart.* London: Orion, 1997.

Slocum, Sally. "Woman the Gatherer: Male Bias in Anthropology." *Toward an Anthropology of Women.* Ed. Raina R. Reiter. New York: Monthly Review Press, 1975. 36-50.

Stott, Rebecca. "The Dark Continent: Africa as Female Body in Haggard's Adventure Fiction." *Feminist Review* 32 (1989): 69-89.

Tepper, Sheri S. *The Enigma Score.* 1987. London: Corgi, 1989.

——. *Raising the Stones.* London: Grafton Books, 1991.

Willis, Connie. *Uncharted Territory.* New York: Bantam, 1994.

Wordsworth, William. "Lines Composed a Few Miles Above Tintern Abbey on Revisiting the Banks of the Wye During a Tour, July 13, 1798." *The Norton Anthology of Poetry,* 3rd edition. Eds., Alexander W. Allison et al. New York: Norton, 1970. 523-26.

Zimmerman, Michael. "Environment." Microsoft ® Encarta ® 98 Encyclopedia: Microsoft, 1998. 1-10.

Loud Achievements:
Lois McMaster Bujold's Science Fiction
Through 1997

1. A Different Kind of Space Opera

Lois McMaster Bujold could well qualify for the title of "Quiet Achiever in 1980s and '90s sf." Between 1985 and 1997 she produced some twelve novels, plus novellas and stories, at the rate of a publication or better a year. Yet when I started this piece as a review of her most recent novel, *Komarr* (1997), the *NYRSF* editor felt Bujold was so little known that most of the references to her *oeuvre* would be unintelligible. Nor, until recently, has she drawn academic attention. The second edition of Clute and Nicholls' *Encyclopedia of Science Fiction* said little about Bujold's work beyond "funny and humane" (171), and many informed readers, male or female, dismiss her along the same lines. It is quite true that she writes unabashed space opera, often classified as military sf, with little overt concern for technology and high emphasis on characters. How, then, has she managed twelve short-listings or final nominations in Hugo, Nebula, and other industry polls, and outright won two Nebulas and four Hugo awards?

Bujold swam into my ken in a manner apparently typical of her work: a specialist bookseller literally handed me *The Warrior's Apprentice* (1986) with a personal recommendation. Being long aware that a female author does not guarantee woman-friendly sf, I took one look at the cover's scantily-clad space bimbo wreathed about another iron-jawed hero, discounted the peculiar seated figure beside them, and nearly said, "No, thanks." But since I trusted Gayle's judgment and was, as usual, looking for new writers, I took a chance. Next evening, I tried the opening pages. The finale of entrance exams for a military academy, callow cadets, imposing men in uniforms. Ho, hum. A perhaps intriguing contrast with the apparent protagonist's "crooked spine," his "too-large-head," and "just-under-five-foot frame" (Bujold, *Apprentice*, 2), an unusual personality hinted by the way he assessed the man-in-uniform's "tricks of body language" (1).

The second page set up a very different resonance:

> The obstacle course… began with a
> concrete wall, five meters high, topped
> with iron spikes. Climbing it would be no
> problem…. it was the coming down that
> worried him (2)

Suddenly the military stomp-and-tromp was twenty years and a galaxy away:

> There was a wall. It did not look
> important. It was built of uncut rocks
> roughly mortared; an adult could look
> over it, and even a child could climb
> it. Where it crossed the roadway it
> degenerated into mere geometry … But

the idea was real.
(Le Guin, *The Dispossessed*, 9)

Even at my first encounter with serious women's sf, let alone feminist sf, it did not need a degree in literature to figure this wall as a multi-level symbol of division between sexist Urras and non-sexist Anarres, between Anarres' stagnant and progressive internal factions, between oppression and freedom on Urras, between futures of isolation and affiliation for both planets. The wall in *Apprentice* seemed less ubiquitous, but it was a symbol too: at first glance, it signified the manifold problems confronting that quirky protagonist en route to his military academy, problems that went beyond physical handicaps to obstacles of birth—his surname Vorkosigan evidently signaled an aristocrat, and he already faced slurs of nepotism—and social stigma. On this planet such an *outre* physique meant genetic mutation, which would once have been a literal kiss of death. "Miles, hey?" thought I, remembering my rudimentary Latin. "If you want to be a soldier, m'lad, you do have miles to go."

At first reading, however, I was sucked into the story by the outrageous consequences of Miles's hyperactive forward momentum, from disaster at the wall—he jumped and broke both legs—to domestic melodrama—he failed the exams, his grandpapa promptly died, and he was caught *in flagrante* by his Da, evidently a person of enormous power and reputation, making out with the current love of his life straight after the funeral. From this *contretemps* he inveigled her, himself, and his spectacularly ugly bodyguard into an incident at a spaceport that left him nominally owner of a decrepit freighter and her pilot, and from there into gun-running to a planetary rebellion, and from that to quondam leadership of a non-existent mercenary fleet, and from that he had to flash home to exoncrate his Da from a charge of treason to the emperor...

Amid this whirlwind I gathered considerable information: the home planet Barrayar was a quasi-feudal, militaristic empire, Miles's Da had been Imperial Regent, and Miles's physical problems sprang from a political drama before he was born. Both were aristocrats committed to democratizing their society—ably assisted by Miles's Mama, a native of aggressively egalitarian but laudably non-sexist and technologically streets-ahead Beta Colony. Miles's suddenly defunct bodyguard evidently had a long pre-history, and Miles himself was an incipient case of schizophrenia as well as chronic hyperactivity. At the close of *Apprentice* his alternate persona as Admiral Naismith was in the closet while Miles finagled his way into the academy, but I had no doubt Naismith would escape to cause more mayhem very soon.

Narrative impulsion is actually a constant in Bujold's work, as is her easy, almost transparent prose style with its occasional unexpected striking turn of phrase—"Death had a temperature and it was damned cold" (*Komarr,* 27)—or its wickedly reshaped allusions: "The cream pie of justice flies one way" (*Vor*, 336). The apparently effortless fluidity of both style and story may actually have militated against critical notice, in comparison to notorious stylists like William Gibson, or, again, Ursula K. Le Guin. But, despite Bujold's space opera plots, the flashes of humor rare either in Le Guin or in sf as a whole, and the steady pigeonholing of her work as military sf, her similarities to Le Guin go far beyond the presence of that wall.

Most obviously, both are consummate character-builders. Indeed, characterization, emphasis on character, and plots that depend on character *and* the novums of technology are among Bujold's strong points. Nowhere does this emerge more clearly than when her work is taken as military sf and compared to that of writers like Jerry Pournelle or David Weber. Bujold can turn a neat paragraph on space weapons' evolution when necessary (*Vor*, 267-68), but her first book, *Shards of Honor* (1986), makes it plain that she means to write about soldiers from the anti-war, pro-people stances common to the peace movement and to many feminists. To Miles's mother Cordelia, young male soldiers are not heroes but "'[p]oor lambs,'" an "'animal sacrifice'" (84). At the most spectacular level, *Shards* rewrites that cliché of sf, space battle. In Niven and Pournelle's well-aged collaboration, *The Mote in God's Eye* (1974), it is sanitized by distance: "lovely to see—ships—like smooth black eggs…drives radiating dazzling light… Scintillations in the black flanks—lines of green and ruby" laser fire (320-21). Extrapolating from Nelson's navy, Weber offers high mortality rates, but dignified deaths. But Bujold extrapolates onward to a space burial detail, confronting the reader with the "reality" of death by decompression: a corpse "spinning fiercely, guts split open—and hanging out in a frozen cascade" (*Shards*, 312).[1]

---

1   As a short story, in 1984 this section of *Shards of Honor* was rejected by the editor of a military sf anthology on the grounds that it was "too gruesome."

The novel also opens with a notable variation on military, and indeed the broader sf tradition, when a minor character is hit by a nerve disruptor. Plenty of minor characters die in sf, with such facility that they have been nicknamed "shreddies." But since Bujold's disruptor disables mentally but does not kill, rather than losing her "shreddie" in decent oblivion, she can drive home the cost of war by making Cordelia tend him through an arduous trek that ends with an uncompromising vision of his future as "an endless series of hospital days as straight and same as a tunnel to the end of his life" (86). Much later, readers must follow Miles into a hospital where his battle casualties are revived from frozen sleep—or not (*Mirror,* 29-37). Repeatedly, Bujold's work shifts focus from the successes, exploits, and glory of war to their human cost.

The differences heighten with Bujold's modification of stock characters. Miles's Da appears in *Shards of Honor* as an apparent clone of that military constant, the heroic space-fleet commander. Like the one in *The Mote in God's Eye*, he suffers military reverses but wins a woman by the novel's end. Unlike Niven and Pournelle's character, however, he turns out to be an ex-lover of the equally military villain. A long way down the saga, Cordelia herself sums him up as, "'bisexual, but subconsciously more attracted to men... Or rather to soldiers... The first time he met me I was in uniform... He thought it was love at first sight'" (*Mirror,* 286). But this innovation is overshadowed by the development of Miles's bodyguard, Sergeant Bothari.

In *Shards of Honor* this "'very complex man with a very limited range of expression, who's had some very bad experiences"' (54) enters as the villain's partly willing tool, a potentially psychopathic torturer, rapist and possibly serial killer. He actually mutates two stock figures from film and fiction, the tough, bullying sergeant of films like *Platoon* (1986) and *Heartbreak Ridge* (1986), and the uncomplicatedly evil villain, the monster, found in horror/thrillers by writers like Dean Koontz. But where Koontz can only glance toward humanizing such a figure, Bujold shapes her monster as a fellow-victim, before, in the scene where he is supposed to rape Cordelia, her own pity makes him her rescuer.

Finding the series at *Apprentice*, I knew little of Bothari before he let himself be shot by another torture victim, whom he still "loved." But if Bujold humanizes, she does not idealize; when I caught up with the pre-history in *Shards of Honor*, the sequence of his "marriage" with this catatonic victim managed the rare feat of evoking repulsion and sympathy at once. It is in *Barrayar* (1991), chronologically earlier but written later, that Bothari expands into the equally rare double of a characterization of high literary subtlety, based on formulaic elements and slotting neatly into a space opera's linear, suspenseful frame.

In *Barrayar*, Bothari's stock bad childhood as a whore's bastard is glanced over, without either exaggeration or sentimentality, while the adult Bothari appears in succession as a true killer, sexually aroused by the prospect of violence, then as midwife for a rescued noblewoman, then, in the climactic scene, as Cordelia's proxy executioner. By the book's close the reader can echo the summary of this "very complex man" with true understanding; yet none of this innovative and complex character-development has impeded the narrative. Among women's interventions in the sf tradition of action/suspense and technical focus, let alone the gung-ho realms of military sf, Bothari's characterization is a *tour de force* that almost overshadows Bujold's long-term development of her central protagonist, Miles Vorkosigan.

Miles bestrides the Vorkosigan universe, a figure whose panache conquers readers as fast as fellow characters and who has bent the shape of the military subgenre along with most of the rules of sf: even as he re-writes the manual for military heroes, Miles slews Bujold's books irrevocably toward the primacy of character. Beyond that, his long-term development is a phenomenon in either mainstream or genre fiction. We are all familiar with the serial hero, from Mulder and Scully to Sherlock Holmes: but how many of them, in the course of their adventures, change and mature, let alone metamorphose? And how many burst generic conventions in the process? On the other hand, mainstream fiction and high literature have traditionally focused on the character and/or development of a protagonist; but how many such writers, from Dickens onward, have taken it beyond a single book?

It is quite easy to see Miles as the focus of Bujold's thematic concerns as a writer, and to propose that those concerns center on the question of identity. Excepting Le Guin, such concerns are uncommon in sf; but they do site Bujold in familiar recent theoretical territory, from the debates of early second-wave feminism to high-flying post-structuralist arguments on the death of the subject and the later, notably post-colonial concentration, on the construction of subjectivity. It is a cliché of early feminist thought that women's subjectivity has been elusive, fractured, and difficult to attain. Later feminists have used post-structuralism to retort that such an argument leans on the passé humanist premise that *anyone* can achieve an unfractured, unproblematic identity. Against such theoretical background, concern with Miles's self-discovery and personality integration can appear slightly dubious; nevertheless, the extended study of such a process in fiction, rather than theory, and what it does to sf and the sf hero, make Miles a *rara avis* well worth following.

2. The Boy Hero Breaks Out

Against Miles's trajectory, Bujold's Vorkosigan *oeuvre* splits easily into two phases, the earlier and later books. Early books are epitomized by *The Warrior's Apprentice*: unabashed space opera, clearly military space opera, with unwonted variations that I have already discussed. Even in *Apprentice*, Bujold's shreddies don't just shred. The death of the pilot officer, tortured for information to allow Miles's first ship capture, is a particularly excruciating case (127-30). Repeatedly, these shards of untoward reality, so to speak, puncture the light-hearted adventure envelope, just as Miles's character repeatedly contradicts what we expect of the classic young male sf protagonist.

In these books Miles appears as what Joan Baez once called Bob Dylan: a "genius brat," a manic loose cannon who triumphs where superiors and enemies fail, an outlaw, a white Coyote prevailing not by gun or fist but wits. Considering his position as a democratic aristocrat, his rebellions against his rank and future status, and his stance on the outside of authority, he also looks a perfect anti-hero. But hardly anything in Jim Villani's description of sf women writers' anti-heroes fits Miles. He is "highly intelligent" but not "rendered impotent by…nature and/or culture" (26). If "not brave in the accepted masculine sense" he is anything but "indecisive," though often "lonely" he is not solitary, and he is above all a "charismatic leader" who does inspire "blind faith" everywhere (27). And unlike Frankenstein or Le Guin's Shevek, his sexuality is definitely not "emasculated" (27-28).

In this subversion of the sf heroic model, the comedy is critical, and although some is drawn by the cultures and other characters, much centers on Miles. Most notably, Bujold makes Miles both comic and able to laugh at himself. Apart from comedies of chaos like *Apprentice*, she often uses his point of view subversively, as in the novella "Labyrinth" (1989), when he is propositioned by the equivalent of an eight-foot virgin female Minotaur. Warned about the downside of lovemaking, she says, "'I have a very high pain threshold,'" to which an appalled Miles's aside is, *"But I don't"* (166).

Such bravado does come at a heavy price. In *Apprentice* Miles doesn't just break his legs, he gets a stomach ulcer and loses his adored Elena to somebody else. The early books highlight the after-effects of his embryonic mishap: brittle bones that break at the slightest stress, ostracism to overcome at home, and untoward interest abroad, as when he nearly ends up in a genetic black-marketer's collection on the Mafia planet of

Jackson's Whole. *Borders of Infinity* (1989), with its three award-winning stories, is strung together by Miles's stay in hospital, as he gets yet another set of arm bones replaced with plastic substitutes. And in "Infinity" itself, his undercover assignment in a prison camp includes an ignominious clothes theft that leaves him naked for a good part of the story, while the successful breakout comes at the cost of a death that haunts him for years.

More central to Bujold's thematic concerns is the fragmenting of Miles's personality between the mercenary Admiral Naismith and the Barrayaran officer Lord Vorkosigan. In the early books Bujold switches with *elan* between the two. After slipping in and out of Naismith's persona in *Apprentice*, in *Brothers in Arms* (1989) Miles infuriates Barrayaran authority, along with their mortal Cetagandan enemies, by making first one, then the other persona his alias. In *The Vor Game* (1990) the same double-bluff runs throughout. In *Cetaganda* (1996) he is limited to Lord Vorkosigan; in *Brothers in Arms*, Bujold ups the stakes by giving Miles a physical double, a clone, whom he acknowledges, in a maternally inherited tradition from Beta Colony, as his true brother. But as the series continues, the strains of the psychic double become more and more evident. Miles invented Naismith, says Cordelia, because Barrayar gave him:

> "so much unbearable stress, so much pain, he created an entire other personality to escape into. He then persuaded several thousand galactic mercenaries to support his psychosis,

> and...conned the Barrayaran Imperium
> into paying for it all." (*Mirror,* 216)

Although his "safety valve" (217) works, Miles needs "the little Admiral" to survive.

As Naismith, Miles is rambunctious, riotous, gung-ho to the point of lunacy. "You mean," says one disbelieving victim in *Apprentice*, "he's like that *all the time*?" (100). His skills in field-command, improvisation, and brilliant skulduggery are strained to the uttermost by his exploits with the Dendarii Free Mercenaries, and only by another sleight-of-hand kept in the service of Barrayar. Naismith reincarnates those notable military figures, Wellington and Napoleon. On the one hand he rivals the Iron Duke at tying a knot and going on amid calamities. On the other, at every opportunity he applies that slogan Napoleon appears to have adapted from Danton: "*L'audace! Toujours l'audace!*" And as Naismith, such bravado serves him well. He prevails in numerous sticky situations, he brings home the goods, and he gets the girl. The problems begin when he wants to take her home as well.

Naismith has no problem with sexuality, at least with women, even if they have wolf's claws and stand eight feet tall. Miles-Naismith's sexuality is, indeed, one of his notable heroic deflections. It takes a very light and daring hand indeed to involve your young hero in a scene of sexual demand—all but harassment—with an eight-foot genetically-enhanced taloned and fanged female soldier whose entering move is to eat a rat alive. It takes a lighter hand to show Miles moved to respond by an ambition for "mountain-climbing" ("Labyrinth," 166) without outrage to the sensibilities of a card-carrying feminist like me. On the other hand, it is a charming renovation of so much heavy-handed sf sex, that when a true siren casts her eye on Miles, he is rescued by a frantic allergy to her perfume—in effect, by a strategic sneeze (*Vor*, 227).

Nevertheless, despite Naismith's heterosexual enterprise, and although Miles's father is quite comfortably credited with bisexuality, as Vorkosigan or Naismith Miles's nearest approach to alternate sexualities is a flirtation with a Beta Colony hermaphrodite. And in the Bujold universe, alternate female sexuality does not appear to exist. But as Lord Vorkosigan, in the early books Miles has no sexual adventures. Indeed, he limits his love interest to vain attempts at making one of his spectacular women into Lady Vorkosigan, a role that they concertedly refuse. His long-term squeeze, the beautiful mercenary Elli Quinn, remarks witheringly that far from becoming a "dirtsucker," she intends to become an Admiral herself (*Mirror,* 25-26). By *Cetaganda* (1996), Lord Vorkosigan is in peril of the fate that threatens Georgette Heyer heroines: being left on the shelf.

By that stage, Miles is also in danger of ossifying as an *enfant terrible*, caught outside the Barrayaran command structure and condemned to rebellious insubordinacy, a brilliant but wacky freelance, a divided personality. A striking divergence, to be sure, from the military sf prototypes and the sf hero or anti-hero, but ultimately, just one more of those adolescent conquerors, from the protagonist of *The Last Starfighter* (1984) back to the Heinlein juveniles, whose entrapment in the light-hearted world of genre sf and space opera will make sure he never grows up. But forestalling this threat comes *Barrayar*. And after it, *Mirror Dance* (1994); and then, *Memory* (1996).

Barrayar opens the later stage of Bujold's *oeuvre*, most obviously because of its quantum jump in power, complexity, and originality, such as the handling of Bothari, and its excursions into women's territory previously untraveled in sf, but also because it initiates a kind of second, deeper pass over the landscape of the earlier books. First, *Barrayar* re-instates a female protagonist; chronologically, it follows *Shards of Honor*, taking Cordelia on from marriage to pregnancy. Second, in Miles's own trajectory it operates uncannily like a regression to the womb, since he spends most of the book in utero—or, more accurately, half in utero and half transferred to a "uterine replicator," one of Bujold's charming examples of woman-centered technology. And having begun Miles's second life in *Barrayar*, Bujold jumps to his literal death in *Mirror Dance*.

Resurrected heroes are not unknown in the non-realist freedom of sf. Few of them, however, happen to be a series protagonist who spends half the novel either deep-frozen or having a heart re-grown in a cryogenic revival clinic, and when he does surface, is handicapped by a bad case of amnesia. In Miles's progress, *Mirror Dance* is actually both a side-step and a necessary preliminary, because it centers on his clone-brother Mark. Originally trained to impersonate Miles and physically warped to match his physique, he was intended as a pawn in the overthrow of the Barrayaran emperor. In *Mirror Dance* Mark gets Miles killed while attempting to match the latter's military prowess in a raid on the clone-factories of his birthplace, Jackson's Whole. With Miles sidelined and literally mislaid for half the novel, Mark is forced to make his own integrations—with Miles's parents, then into the Vorkosigan family and Barrayaran society—and then, when he returns to Jackson's Whole to find Miles, his disintegration, as his personality fragments under the tortures of a mutual enemy. The novel closes after some normal fast and twisty action with Miles recovered—in both senses—and Mark's personality reconciled, its dark aspects accepted along with his abnormal physique, and his own interests laid down within his individual niche on Barrayar.

Mirror Dance, then, is a double reach for psychic equilibrium: for Miles with his physical double, for Mark with the unstable, as yet undefined and often dark limits of his own subjectivity. If the end leaves Mark as a close approximation of the monolithic humanist subject, Miles takes away more dangerous mementos than a fresh collection of scars and another beautiful but transient lover. His resurrection also leaves him with chronic, sudden, unpredictable convulsions that threaten not only his persona as Admiral Naismith but also his entire military career. It is this "death" and its associated casualties that occupy *Memory*.

Bujold once remarked that her plots are often predicated on "the worst possible thing you [could] do" to a character (Counihan, 22). For Miles as Naismith *or* Vorkosigan, the worst thing that could ever happen is to be expelled from the Barrayaran military and his niche in ImpSec, the elite if invisible crème of Barrayaran security. It is not unusual for military sf heroes to be disgraced or expelled from service, even to have the expulsion carried over a couple of books, as with David Weber's Honor Harrington. But in these cases, the disgrace is always falsely based. In *Memory* it is not only real but permanent: Miles is found out fudging a report to cover the effects of a convulsion during action, and after an excruciating scene with the head of ImpSec, also an old family friend and mentor, he is pitched literally and metaphorically into the street.

The spy-novel plot that carries *Memory* exhibits Bujold's usual narrative drive and ingenuity; but in Miles's ongoing story it is only a springboard for this metaphorical death of his career, and more crucially, of his Naismith persona. Naismith can only function in the mercenary fleet, and the mercenary fleet freelances for ImpSec. But to take the fleet and become Naismith permanently would be to commit treason, and thus kill, perhaps in the most literal sense, Lord Vorkosigan. Bujold's solution also springs from the spy-plot, but it is a plotter's stroke of genius. Miles is dragged from the slough of despair to rescue the man who sacked him, after the latter suffers amnesia and derangement from a deteriorating memory chip; the only leverage adequate to the task is to overleap the ranks of Lord Vorkosigan or Naismith, or even his father: he gets himself appointed a kind of supreme troubleshooter-cum-Viceroy, an Imperial Auditor. At the novel's close, the appointment is made permanent.

Despite this ultimate victory, much of *Memory* operates as a long goodbye to Miles's previous glories. He loses all three women, Elli, Elena, and his wolf-soldier, Sergeant Taura, who have been lovers or loved. He revisits the site of past loss and victory in "The Mountains of Mourning" (1989) and finds it empty too. He has destroyed his official military career, and, in effect, chosen to excise half his personality. At the novel's close, he is alone in the empty family mansion with nothing but a bottle and the consciousness that he has survived the worst traumas of his traumatic life, along with its worst temptation: to sell himself for reinstatement in ImpSec. In the process, he has reached a moment of almost pure humanist self-resolution, when he decides, amid the tortures of loss and un-direction, that "I elect to be…myself" (387).

In force and intensity as well as this elegiac undertone, *Memory* is indeed a quantum jump ahead of *The Warrior's Apprentice*, although in Miles's double trajectory it fills the same position of excursion from childhood and foundation of a new personality. But where Mark subsumes and reconciles himself to his dark internal Others, Miles's integration is achieved by an excision—or, as Bujold has put it, a "repossession" ("Letterspace," Letter 8), with all the word's overtones, theological as well as financial—and a metamorphosis at very high cost. Nor is the cost limited to the characters. Reading *Memory*, I myself felt very much like Wordsworth seems to have when he wrote "Ode on the Intimations of Immortality": what we had here was remarkable, spectacular, far more powerful than *Apprentice* and its ilk, but it was also darker, less sparkling, without that adolescent, outrageous *joie d'esprit*. The protestations of a past not missed fell a little hollowly on the ear. In fact, another Australian specialist bookseller remarked to me that he was a little deterred by Bujold's later work, because it was "so serious."

Memory does foreshadow a daring push beyond the limits of military sf and indeed of sf in general. The boy hero is more than growing up, he has burst from his chrysalis, and Bujold is shifting him clear out of the military ambience that had underwritten his appeal to the readership. And sf readers, whether of military or other sub-genres, have made it very clear, as with Samuel R. Delany's later books or Patricia Anthony's remarkable Alien novels, that they know what they want, and they don't want too much character, and they don't want too much experimentation, and they're not too keen on anything but good old adventure fiction (McGuirk, 126) plots. Yet despite this firmly living tradition, even despite Bujold's reputed obscurity, *Barrayar* and *Mirror Dance* both won their year's Hugo, and *Barrayar* made the Nebula final nominations as well, while *Memory*, so much darker and even more different, still made the final ballots of both the Hugo and Nebula awards.

3. Growing Up Miles

Komarr begins to unfold the new personality *Memory* heralded. As a civilian, Miles experiences pangs of nostalgia, but he also appears at once more subdued and more redoubtable than before. Bujold grew the emperor Gregor up between the troubled adolescent of *The Vor Game* and the redoubtable judge of men in *Mirror Dance*. *Komarr* offers the grown-up Miles. It also offers another first for a Vorkosigan book, a viewpoint split between Miles and a female protagonist, and for conveying the change in Miles this double viewpoint is highly effective. When Miles enters *Komarr* through Ekaterin Vorsoisson's eyes, it gave me a startled sense of seeing him for the first time. There have been peepholes of outer perspective throughout the series: Miles's contemplation of his scars in a mirror, or a video clip of him next to Mark. But as a long-term reader I know him as young officer, adolescent, genius brat—even embryo. To Ekaterin, however, he has never been anything but an Imperial Auditor. He thus acquires an instant new stature to match his expanded personality; not to mention, since she first gauges his height as "speaking to her cleavage" (7), another instant adult status. For the first time, Lord Vorkosigan rather than Admiral Naismith appears as a sexual being.

This jump is strengthened by another expansion: finally, Miles has met a woman whose ambitions might just include becoming Lady Vorkosigan; in fact, it appears that Miles has Met His Fate, and its winning will not be easy. Predictably, she is not a stock love object, neither a siren nor a Vor virgin nor a brilliant military officer, but an unhappily married bureaucrat's wife. The developing relationship emerges not as the *coup de foudre* of sexual passion or the giddy gavotte of teenagers' mating, but as a rapprochement between two equally scarred, equally wary people, with mutual attraction but reciprocal embarrassments and vulnerabilities. After the vintage Bujold comedy where they land in a lake together during a superfluous rescue attempt, Ekaterin sees Miles undressed, a revelation of scars as well as warped physique, and then suffering a convulsion. When he is ambushed by the villains, she has to rescue him. Meanwhile Miles rifles her computer files and overhears her second marriage proposal, sees her boorish husband put her down, and witnesses the violation of privacy when ImpSec fast-penta and interrogate her over his death. Ekaterin emerges as a fitting match for this new Miles, more constricted by past and upbringing than his mother Cordelia, but cool, resourceful, independent, and the agent of the villains' final defeat. Moreover, in the closing scene she manages yet another first for a Vorkosigan book: she actually silences Miles.

Komarr ends rather than closes, as all the books in the second phase do, this time with Miles established in his non-military career, but in hot pursuit of marriage rather than a love affair. If you apply the classic psychoanalytic schema, he now appears a proper Freudian subject whom the series has taken from infancy to adulthood, integrating a fragmented personality, activating his superego, moving out of both his father's shadow—Miles carefully points out that *he* was never an Imperial Auditor (*Memory*, 447)—and his mother's lightly sketched ascendancy—she guesses wrongly over his choice between Naismith and Vorkosigan (319). Finding a mate will complete the trajectory. I can think of no other sf characterization that combines such appeal with such a sustained and complex development, far less such an expansion of generic boundaries. Miles alone makes Bujold worthy of comparison with Le Guin.

4. "Codedly Feminine"

Like the wall in *Apprentice*, Miles is more than he originally seems. When I first began analyzing the Bujold books, Miles's physical fragility, his height, his inability to use physical strength and violence, quickly recalled Robin Roberts' concept of the codedly feminine: a process where "an author ...explores a singularly feminine dilemma using a male character as stand-in, or cover"(16). I was charmed to find Bujold herself calling Miles a "female in disguise," and "socially disadvantaged" by his physique, "just as women in patriarchal society are made to feel deformed" (Lake, 8). In this light, the wall in *Apprentice* instantly assumed an extra significance; like the wall in *The Dispossessed,* it also symbolized gender bars. I recalled, too, Le Guin writing of her "private delight" in one of her most famous characters, the Getheni Estraven from *The Left Hand of Darkness*, "not a man, but a manwoman," who usurped male roles ("Redux," 15). Estraven, however, is ambiguously gendered, not codedly feminine. But Miles's exploits read very easily as women's solutions to the problems of a masculinist world, including military space opera. Repeatedly, from *Apprentice* on, Miles appears as physically weaker, more fragile than his opponents; and he prevails by intelligence as well as audacity, by manipulation and psychic judo as well as forward momentum. In a further judo turn, female readers accustomed to taking on male identification find themselves identifying with a man who really *is* one of them.

The codedly feminine in Bujold's work does not stop with Miles. I once proposed ("Letterspace," Letter 3) that Miles and Mark are Take One and Take Two of the concept: like Estraven, Miles achieves all the masculine things that women would *like* to do. He wins by wits and keeps charity, lacks muscle and still manages to manipulate, leads on battlefields and can salvage lost causes by charisma alone. In the early books he is manic, intellectually brilliant, yet keeps compassion and sensitivity, for example in the way he always feels for his dead. But for all his accompanying problems, Miles is the daylight version of the codedly feminine.

Mark is the night-time version: the codedly feminine that women do *not* like to face. To start with his body, he is forced into an unnatural shape, but not by accident, and he suffers that eternal women's problem of weight. In *Mirror Dance* he exhibits the normally female eating disorder, bulimia,[2] and in the throes of his refusal to play Miles, he uses it as a weapon of defense. It has been argued that many anorexics actually control their bodies to thwart social demand. Nor does Mark ever make a success of charisma, leadership, and field command. In fact, in finding himself he renounces all traffic with the military. Moreover, Mark suffers for most of *Mirror Dance* from self-hate, hideously low self-esteem, and masochism, all proverbial women's psychic problems.

Beyond this, *Mirror Dance* gives Mark a clear case of Multiple Personality Disorder, another classic women's problem, and again, it operates in his favor. It is intrigu-

---

2   I am indebted to Tess Williams for first pointing this out to me.

ing to set this fictional construction against the incident discussed by Allucquere Rosanne Stone (1995), where a rapist tried for assaulting an MPD sufferer was convicted on the grounds that in her other personality she was not entirely responsible. But disorders like MPD are also a form of the madness that has haunted women throughout history, holding over them the threat of wrongful commitment, if not the domestic asylum sketched in Charlotte Perkins Gilman's now classic feminist text, "The Yellow Wallpaper" (1892).

In addition to these "women's" problems, it is Mark who suffers the truly horrendous childhood, for despite Miles's physical disabilities and trials with doctors, he is not abused, and he has an amplitude of love. As a result, it is Mark who displays the hate and rancor and envy that women are culturally conditioned to suppress from the day they read "Cinderella" in nursery school. Such negative emotions are socially unacceptable even among feminists, who have long discussed the questions of women's rage and violence. But what truly situates Mark on the night side of the codedly feminine is that, unlike Miles, Mark is not only trained as an assassin but also, lacking Miles's brittle bones, he can kill: physically. Hand to hand.

Female violence invokes enormous social pressure, as evidenced by the reaction of sf critics like William Schuyler to the killing of the male Boss by Russ's assassin in *The Female Man* (1975). Schuyler could only explain it by considering Jael mad (85). In contrast, Mark's brutal hand-to-hand killing in *Mirror Dance* has attracted no censure. Why? Because the victim is patently evil, or because, for a codedly feminine male, physical violence is quite all right? The implicit veto on women's violence does prevail throughout Bujold's work. Although Cordelia can rough up and tie down her infuriating psychiatrist in *Shards of Honor*, and Elli Quinn or Elena can break vexing men's limbs or kill in battle, it takes the purely evil Cavilo, in *The Vor Game*, to use a weapon in cold blood.

When I tried this reading of Miles and Mark on Bujold, she replied, "Did I also mention that Mark is going to end up a *very* rich man? And women are discouraged from paying attention to money, too . . ." ("Letterspace," Letter 4).

5. Bujold's Female Characters

If Miles and Mark offer striking examples of a codedly feminine male character, a suppressed feminism that echoes Le Guin's manwoman, Bujold also parallels Le Guin in writing about male protagonists because "malestuff is easier to do" (Lake, 9). Le Guin found it difficult to write about women until the mid '70s. "What I needed was…feminism" ("Fisherwoman," 234). Only in the wake of her most famous novels, such as *The Dispossessed* and *The Left Hand of Darkness*, does Le Guin produce female protagonists. In Bujold's work, however, the masculine military world of Barrayar is undercut not only by codedly feminine figures like Miles and Mark, but by clear incursions of what Bujold calls "femalestuff" (Lake, 9). This "stuff" is most often a novel with an outright female protagonist that deals openly with female rather than feminine problems. Like Le Guin, Bujold found it "requires deeper and more original thought" than "'malestuff'" (Lake, 9) and again, it follows a double trajectory, opening with *Shards of Honor*, recurring with *Barrayar*, and expanding with *Komarr*, where the double male/female viewpoint puts male and femalestuff side by side.

As later books give the deeper, less acceptable but more powerful versions of identity problems and of the codedly feminine, so femalestuff through the series deepens and moves toward the night-time side. In *Shards of Honor*, Cordelia encounters the dangers of war, imprisonment, torture by the enemy, and misunderstanding and potential imprisonment by her own side. In all this, however, she functions as the clean and upright if remarkable version of the female hero, a figure spreading through sf in the wake of feminism. To sum up a long and complex argument, such heroes can be read as figures in tension between competing elements. On one side is the Amazon, the woman-centered warrior that Joanna Russ's Alyx freed from the sword-and-sorcery genre, who is at base "independent of men" (Lefanu, 34). At its most feminist this element produces Marion Zimmer Bradley's Free Amazons, Suzy McKee Charnas's Riding Women in *Motherlines* (1978), and Nicola Griffith's farmers and nomads in *Ammonite* (1993). On the other side, the discourse of gender equality derived from liberal feminism, used in sf by both men and women writers, produces the rough, tough, unquestioningly heterosexual female hero who proves herself by out-fighting, out-drinking, and out-bedding men. Variants fill the sf continuum, from Heinlein's Friday through Piserchia's girlish Jade in *Star Rider* (1974) to Ripley in the *Alien* movies and John Varley's more sexually flexible Cirocco Jones.

In *Shards of Honor* Cordelia presents a remarkable combination of the two strands. "'[A]s professional as any officer I've ever served with, without once trying be an, an imitation man'" (58). Ethically determined to protest war and preserve life, she can still command a ship, wield a stunner, spin a nifty lie, and anticipate the men in heading off a mutiny. Foreshadowing Miles's development, however, she replaces Cirocco's physical toughness with wits. Sub-sets of this female hero appear with Elli Quinn, Sergeant Taura, and Elena Bothari -Jesek, Miles's first love. Elli is probably the closest to stock: even though she appears first as a casualty with her face blasted off by laser fire, then stunningly re-modeled, she remains the tough, efficient, forthrightly sexy mercenary, the woman many '60s and '70s liberal feminists would have liked to be. Taura, with her ge-netic abnormalities, is a more original and complicat-ed variation: a killer who can rout men with a stare, but also Miles's rowdy long-term lover, who thinks to put on pink "claw-polish" to raid the Jackson's Whole crèche so she won't scare the clone-children (*Mirror,* 81). But Taura also shares the oldest male military mys-tique, for she is going, like Achilles himself, to die very young. Much of the pathos in Miles's final farewell to Taura is that he is losing her to death rather than part-ing alone.

Elena extends the military female hero furthest: Sergeant Bothari's daughter, barred from the military on sexist Barrayar, she becomes a superbly efficient galactic mercenary. Miles's first love, she marries his future fleet's engineer. In *The Warrior's Apprentice* she also sketches the woman's story of discovering and reconciling with an alienated mother. In *Mirror Dance* an equally brief sketch shows her coming to terms with her father's complex past along with Barrayar. And in *Memory*, another episode recapitulates the main plot, as Elena and her husband leave the mercenary fleet because Elena is finished soldiering. "'I've proved Barrayar wrong. I've been a soldier, and a damn good one." Now "'I want to find out who *else* I can be'" (*Memory*, 21).

With *Barrayar*, written eight years after *Shards*, "to grow in power and control before I could do justice to [its] themes" (Lake, 8), Bujold moves into darker aspects of femalestuff, notably with pregnancy. In an early reading of one scene, "I never mentioned hemorrhage anywhere…yet every female listener reported thinking about hemorrhage at exactly the point I intended them to" (Lake, 7). Such biological femalestuff is rare in sf, beyond the work of Marion Zimmer Bradley. Bradley herself repeats a comment that, "'You can always tell a Bradley story—someone has a baby'" ("Responsibilities," 29). But Bradley tends to elide "all the complications of pregnancy and childbirth that women think of every day during the nine months" (Lake, 7). Let alone the nightmares of finding the child imperfect, learning that your father-in-law wants it aborted, and having the embryo stolen by a political enemy. The worst thing happens to Cordelia as a birthing mother in *Barrayar*, not once but several times over. But Bujold neatly dodges Bradley's problems in *Darkover Landfall* (1972), where the use of anti-abortion discourse drew heavy critiques from feminist critics and fans of sf. In *Barrayar* Cordelia fights against aborting Miles, which allows Bujold to duck the thornier problem of whether an abortion should be done.

Though two women do have babies in Barrayar, neither Bujold nor her women accept Bradley's Darkovan saw that "the world will go as it will, and not as you or I will have it." Cordelia saves Miles with the Betan technology of the uterine replicator, then by a rescue raid in defiance of her husband, then by having Bothari execute the usurper on her order. She also has a female support system: the noblewoman whose baby Bothari delivers has befriended her, and her female bodyguard guides the palace raid. Finally, the most powerful femalestuff of the novel is the scene where the fate of Barrayar is decided as Cordelia and the child emperor's captive mother trade the whereabouts of their sons.

Yet despite the Hugo that implies reader approval and Bujold's intent to write more femalestuff (Lake, 9), the series' structure has marginalized Cordelia, as *The Warrior's Apprentice* was followed by *Brothers in Arms*, *Borders of Infinity*, and *The Vor Game*, and as *Barrayar* was succeeded by *Mirror Dance* and *Memory*. With Miles not merely developed but metamorphosed, any further femalestuff demanded a new female protagonist from outside Miles's family and optimally, to provide Miles's adult, non-transient love interest. All these options, and a new expansion of femalestuff, appear with Ekaterin Vorsoisson in *Komarr*.

The new expansion is a first for Bujold, but not for the genre. What is sometimes called domestic sf has been flitting through the field since Gernsback's day:

women's stories mostly, scorned by the cognoscenti (which sometimes includes feminists), rarely long in print, their tone resolutely unheroic, their focus determinedly on the nuts and bolts of not-so-everyday life. The classics include stories like Mildred Clingerman's "The Minister Without Portfolio." Connie Willis does the update: housing problems on a space station, the double-joke of aliens who appear on Earth as normally nerdy human scientists ("Spice Pogrom," "And Come from Miles Around"). But this approach naturally militates against the high-gravity, save-the-universe tone of most sf; to combine them without leaving the seams rucked awkwardly between the two is one of the genre's hardest challenges. *Komarr* does it remarkably well. More remarkably, *Komarr* does it structurally, by splitting the viewpoint between Miles and Ekaterin.

This split domesticates sf at a level previously inaccessible to Bujold's fiction, where home life was either the elevated milieu of Vorkosigan House or the space-Utopia of Beta Colony. In *Komarr*, the woman's view provides the off-Earth equivalent of a posted US army family: school-age son, colonial bureaucrat husband, non-working wife. Except that on Komarr, middle-class mundanities, like grocery shopping, putting up guests, taking the kids to school, are inexorably warped by the sf setting. On Komarr, you hire gravity beds, live in oxygen domes, buy vat-grown meat, and visit the countryside in a breather mask. This exotic domesticity simultaneously defamiliarizes the on-Earth parallel and highlights the alternating scenes of scientific investigation and thriller violence.

The real depth of the femalestuff, however, plumbs a social rather than biological woman's battlefield at a level few mainstream novels have reached. The scenes between Ekaterin and her husband illuminate a loveless marriage to its nadir: not merely the squabbles, the endemic disagreements, the bitter strains of mismanagement or failed ambition, the public putdowns and social embarrassments, but also the ghastly apparatus of loveless sex. When Ekaterin has to "study Tien warily" and decide "she had better offer sex very soon" because "it was past time to defuse him" (*Komarr,* 55), Bujold replaces the potential glamour of any sex-in-space with the excruciating truth of many mundane relationships; worst of all is the reader's understanding that this *is* normal for the marriage.

Beyond this gritty re-vision of yet another social myth, *Komarr* offers the uncodedly female version of the metamorphoses in *Memory* and *Mirror Dance.* Ekaterin enters the novel as an unhappily married wife, with a son threatened by her husband's heritable genetic problem. She leaves a widow with a cured child, a firm ambition, and strong prospects for a future career in landscaping, from gardens to planets, plus the kudos of having prevented disaster to both Komarr and Barrayar. This picture of a woman struggling from a chrysalis of stagnation to begin a second life is a staple of feminist fiction, including sf like Sheri S. Tepper's *Grass* (1989): it is a metamorphosis as arduous as Miles's, from a suffocating life into one that, however painful the transit, at least promises to be free.

6. Bujold's "Covert Feminism"

The femalestuff in *Komarr* recalls Le Guin's later 1970s works, which so often center on female protagonists who take giant strides into an independent if unsafe unknown, as in "The New Atlantis" (1975) or *The Eye of the Heron* (1978). Such femalestuff is obviously related to second-wave feminism, but here the two writers do, ostensibly, part company. Although *The Left Hand of Darkness* was a landmark in feminist sf, it was only in the mid and later '70s that Le Guin openly espoused feminism, a shift clear in the two versions of her well-known essay "Is Gender Necessary?" Once "out," however, Le Guin's feminism was forthright and overt, characteristic of the '60s and '70s, when feminism was as much a political stance as a source of fictional ideas. Bujold, on the other hand, began publishing in the '80s, when feminism in the US had been driven underground by political reverses and internal fragmentation, reverses that mark writers as well. Joan Gordon takes Connie Willis, Karen Joy Fowler, and Sheri S. Tepper as examples of '80s writers who subsume rather than preach feminism, calling their work "post feminist crypsi sf" (5), a term that could cover Bujold too.

When pushed, Bujold will defend her covert feminism on the grounds that "[n]o feminist, writing a feminist tract" can "change any man's—fixed mind" but that "a book packaged as militarist sf" might bring in "alien ideas" unnoticed (Lake, 9). But her need to stress the female aspects of her work suggests that male readers ignore these elements. In fact, they compliment her on "writing like a man" (7), a phrase that must throw her subversive claim into serious doubt. Like Willis, who disavows feminism (Gordon, 5), Bujold would rather "call myself a human beingist" (Lake, 9). Her published credo includes "to journey from the self to the other is an improvement… People are more important than things— Good and evil are only meaningful as a quality of individuals possessing free will" (11).

Against the current (feminist) theoretical field, these unremarkable statements proclaim what is called, with varying degrees of disapproval, classic liberalism: that is, the philosophic fountainhead of individualism, but also of crusades for human rights. And from the Seneca Falls Declaration of Sentiments to the foundation of NOW, such thought has also been a constant in feminism. Indeed, in what Katie King calls "taxonomies of feminism" (124) the hegemonic divergence falls between the liberal-heterosexual and radical-lesbian axes of thought and action, prefigured in the late '60s gap between NOW and the more radical organization of WLM. It reappears in feminist sf with those two founding mothers, Le Guin and Joanna Russ. Though both are white, middle-class, tertiary-educated feminists, Le Guin's work follows a '60s liberal trajectory from race to gender issues, picking up later essentialist feminist viewpoints and contending throughout with the liberal bias to individualism. Russ, on the other hand, brilliantly anticipates historical trends with the production of radical and lesbian perspectives; yet like radical feminism proper, that explosion of thought and action in the late '60s to early '70s, she almost burned out before the '70s' end.

Given this perspective, Bujold aligns immediately with Le Guin, not simply for her liberal manifesto but because all her notable expansions of femalestuff are unquestioningly and entirely heterosexually based. As I mentioned, although male bisexuals and hermaphrodites appear, the Vorkosigan universe has no hint of lesbians. Moreover, as Le Guin moved in the '80s toward what is now called essentialist feminism, with its monolithic oppositions of "Men" and "Women," not a few of Bujold's remarks point the same way. Beyond the unshaded dichotomy of male and femalestuff, there are remarks like "everything I've written is by definition through female eyes" (Lake, 9). And if male readers miss these nuances, "I don't write like a man, you just read like one" (8). In feminist theoretical circles, even in the early '80s, such blanket statements would have drawn fast questions like, Which female? White, black, middle-class, working class, Third World, First World, straight, lesbian? The lessons against universalizing that (white straight) feminists learnt in the early '80s have long precluded such claims.

Moreover, for some feminists, liberalism and its ties to individualism, and thence, less happily, to capitalism, are actually a handicap. To Sarah Lefanu, Le Guin's earlier and most famous male protagonists are "a dead weight in the centre of the novels," because they are "caught in the stranglehold of liberal individualism" (137). And the feminist philosopher Andrea Nye considers liberalism inherently masculinist (526); to such feminist thinking, which has produced some of the most devastating critiques of Le Guin's work, her very emphasis on character, so laudable in the sf context, is a political weakness, while crusades such as the Civil Rights campaign and the ongoing feminist initiatives that her work has engaged since the early '60s, are themselves tainted with the flavor of liberalism.

This stance is strongly influenced by radical and lesbian feminist thought, to use the commonest terminology, and it too has produced problems, most notably the hardening of universalist and ultimately dubious attempts to valorize women in terms of traditionally feminine attributes. The limits of liberal-heterosexual thought do emerge clearly, however, from critiques of Le Guin's work for the absence of alternate sexualities, and the assumptions that undercut even such Utopian societies as Anarres, where Shevek's career-focused mother is seen as cruel and cold, in direct contradiction of the gender-equality supposedly prevalent. Such critiques can be leveled at Bujold, if not directly for her depictions of women: while the charge of hegemonic heterosexuality may appear narrow or special-pleading, its consequences do not stop with the absence of lesbians on Barrayar. Liberal-heterosexual has usually taken white as its third cluster-term; and the blindness to class and sexuality of '70s feminists produced racism that extended from black to Third World women. The same racial myopia marks the Vorkosigan universe. While there is a vestigial echo of the long-lived US/Russian opposition in the siting of Barrayar, with its Cyrillic alphabet, its harsh world, savage history, and quasi-feudal society, against the glossy but flawed democracy of "galactics" like Beta Colony, on Barrayar itself there appear to be no racial tensions. Hillmen and city men may jeer at each other, districts may be backward and ethnic minorities preserved in a Greek dialect, but of ethnic enclaves, racial or even religious tensions, Barrayar appears remarkably free. One can argue they were all stamped out during the Time of Isolation or the ferocious Cetagandan war, but this too appears something of a special plea. Despite its savage past and sexist present, Barrayar may well be, as Bujold herself once suggested, the "white-bread suburb of the galaxy" ("Letterspace," Letter 4).

For me this liberal-based myopia surfaces notably in *Komarr*, with a kneejerk response to some of the imperial ideology. As the series opens, Komarr appears a hostile equal, whose perfidy in letting the Cetagandans invade Barrayar unresisted, and whose geographic position astride Barrayar's one outlet to the wider galaxy "forced" its conquest. By *Komarr* this status has insensibly eroded into the more orthodox position of subtly inferior colony. The Komarran freedom fighters are either warped to lunacy, as in *Brothers in Arms*, or in *Komarr*, both disastrously short-sighted and mildly ludicrous. This begins to invoke the specter of live US imperialism; and as an Australian, at once colonizer and colonized, my hackles rise at some of Miles's comments about foolish rebels who ought to know a benevolent tyranny when they see one. Miles and his emperor may Mean Well, but at my gut-level, Good Guys are not colonizers.

Such flaws invoke feminist standpoint theory, developed notably by Nancy Hartsock and Donna Haraway, which conscripted Marx's claim that only those under a system see it with clarity, to argue that only women could see their oppression clearly. Less happily, this paved the way for more essentialist claims that only women, by virtue of their bare biological status, could perceive "the truth." It has been more usefully modified by Sandra Harding, who argued that if feminism is to make any difference, it must posit that men can learn from women's picture of them, just as white feminists learnt from the critiques of blacks, middle-class women from working-class women, and so on. The crucial point is that to modify the top-down standpoint, it is necessary to re-invent that hegemonic Self as Other. And while Bujold has made remarkable innovations in the enduring masculinist traditions of sf and military sf, such self-subversion has not yet begun to emerge.

These are sins of omission rather than commission; they are balanced by Bujold's expansions and innovations in the field, just as her covert feminism is balanced by accomplished examples of feminist strategy in recuperating myths, as in her cross of Ariadne and Andromeda in "Labyrinth." Moreover, if "there are no Utopias without women" (Fitting, 107), *Ethan of Athos* (1986) constructs a glimpse of a gay culture/ world whose sole female presence is donated ovaries, yet whose protagonist comes to modify his stereotype of women in his adventures elsewhere. This is balanced by the sketch in *Shards of Honor* of Beta Colony, a liberal-heterosexual Utopia where men and women share armed service, uterine replicators allow reproduction in vivo or in vitro, girls' ears and hymens are pierced at puberty, and hermaphrodites live next to licensed sexual therapists.

Moreover, despite the repeated criticism that Bujold has little interest in technology or much use for that hoary sf shibboleth, big ideas, one could hardly ask for bigger ideas, or more smoothly assimilated science, than the terraforming scheme that underpins the plot in *Komarr*. Nor, if sf's mandate is to extrapolate (scientific) ideas in their social context, could one ask for a more fascinating example than the long-term impact on Barrayar of the uterine replicator, whose consequences ramify throughout the three most recent books. Young men left unmarried because their parents wanted only sons so there is a dearth of girls, class structures fraying as Vor aristocrats have to marry low-class girls, women dictating the marriage terms depending on whether the husband will sanction use of the replicator… As Cordelia remarks, "'About half a generation from now, [the Vor system is] not going to know what hit it'" (*Mirror,* 297). This is social experiment on a truly ample scale; if it has gathered little interest, it may be because of that equally hoary prejudice against ideas that are neither hard science nor men-based.

Given this plethora of innovative and formula-shaking sf, one wonders why Bujold remains obscure; especially when that list of short-lists and final nominations includes two novels that topped the *Locus* poll for best sf novel in the last five years. If the cognoscenti aren't voting for Bujold, then who is reading *Locus*? If the cognoscenti are reading *Locus*, then why does Bujold appear to be relatively unknown? And are none of the cognoscenti academics, or has she, like feminist sf as a whole, fallen into the crack between the canon of male writers who attract male (and female) critics, and the even smaller canon of feminist writers who attract academic criticism? I could quote Helen Merrick at length on the intersections of mainstream and sf criticism and the Black Hole at their intersection into which Marleen Barr also thinks feminist sf (or fabulation, in her terms) has fallen. Or I could point out that many feminist academics draw their knowledge of sf from lines like the Women's Press, and suggest that because her feminism is covert they consider Bujold a man's author, while sf academics aren't always interested in feminism, and a large number of them are men, who consider Bujold a woman's author. Whichever way it falls, this neglect seems as surprising as it is inexplicable. If all else fails, one can only hope that somewhere out there a legion of Bujold readers are now pressing books into the hands of unsuspecting others and urging, "Read this!" So that the wall of silence will be surmounted, if not in Miles' inimitable fashion, then some day very soon.

Works Cited

Barr, Marleen S. *Lost in Space: Probing Feminist Science Fiction and Beyond.* Chapel Hill: University of North Carolina Press, 1993.

Bradley, Marion Zimmer. "Responsibilities and Temptations of Women Science Fiction Writers." *Women Worldwalkers: New Dimensions of Science Fiction and Fantasy,* Ed. Jane B. Weedman. Lubbock: Texas Technical Institute, 1985. 25-42.

Bujold, Lois McMaster. *Barrayar.* New York: Baen, 1991.

——. *Borders of Infinity.* 1989. New York: Baen, 1991.

——. "The Borders of Infinity." *Borders of Infinity.* 1989. New York: Baen, 1991. 215-307.

——. *Brothers in Arms.* 1989. London: Headline, 1990.

——. *Cetaganda.* New York: Baen, 1996.

——. *Ethan of Athos.* 1986. London: Headline, 1989.

——. *Komarr.* New York: Baen, 1997.

——. "Labyrinth." 1989. *Borders of Infinity.* 1989. New York: Baen, 1991. 103-211.

——. *Memory.* New York: Baen, 1996.

——. *Mirror Dance.* 1994. New York: Baen, 1995.

——. "The Mountains of Mourning." *Borders of Infinity.* 1989. New York: Baen, 1991. 9-100.

——. *Shards of Honor.* 1986. New York: Baen, 1993.

——. *The Vor Game.* New York: Baen, 1990.

——. *The Warrior's Apprentice.* 1986. New York: Baen, 1988.

Bujold, Lois, and Sylvia Kelso. "Letterspace." *Women of Other Worlds: excursions through science fiction and feminism,* Eds. Helen Merrick and Tess Williams. Perth: University of West Australia Press, 1999. 383-409.

Counihan, Elizabeth. "The Worst Possible Thing." *Interzone,* November (1995): 20-23.

Clute, John, and Peter Nicholls, Eds. *The Encyclopedia of Science Fiction.* 2nd ed. London: Orbit, 1993.

Fitting, Peter. "For Men Only: A Guide to Reading Single-sex Worlds." *Women's Studies* 14 (1987): 101-17.

Gordon, Joan. "Connie Willis's Doomsday for
Feminism: Doomsday Book by Connie Willis."
New York Review of Science Fiction June (1993): 4-5.

Harding, Sandra. "Reinventing Ourselves as Other:
More New Agents of History and Knowledge."
American Feminist Thought at Century's End: A Reader.
Ed. Linda S. Kauffman. Cambridge MA, Oxford
UK: Blackwell, 1993. 140-64.

Haraway, Donna. "Situated Knowledges: The Science
Question in Feminism and the Privilege of Partial
Perspectives." *Feminist Studies* 14.3 (1988): 575-99.

Hartsock, Nancy. "The Feminist Standpoint:
Developing the Ground for a Specifically
Feminist Historical Materialism." *Feminism and
Methodology: Social Science Issues.* Ed. Sandra Harding:
Bloomington: Indiana University Press, 1987. 157-
80.

King, Katie. *Theory in its Feminist Travels: Conversations
in U.S. Women's Movements.* Bloomington: Indiana
University Press, 1994.

Lake, Ken. Interview with Lois McMaster Bujold.
Vector February/March (1993): 7-11.

Le Guin, Ursula K. *Dancing at the Edge of the World:
Thoughts On Words, Women, Places.* 1989. New York:
Harper and Row, 1990.

——. *The Dispossessed.* 1974. St. Albans: Panther, 1975.

——. *The Eye of the Heron.* 1978. *The Eye of the Heron
and Other Stories.* Ed. Virginia Kidd. St. Albans:
Panther, 1980. 209-51.

——. "The Fisherwoman's Daughter." Le Guin, *Dancing* 212-37.

——. "Is Gender Necessary?" 1976. *The Language of the Night: Essays on Fantasy and Science Fiction.* Ed. Susan Wood. New York: Perigee, 1977. 161-69.

—— "Is Gender Necessary? Redux." 1976/1987. Le Guin, *Dancing* 7-16.

——. *The Left Hand of Darkness.* 1969. St. Albans: Panther, 1973.

——. "The New Atlantis." 1975. *The Compass Rose.* London: Granada, 1984. 20-48.

Lefanu, Sarah. *In the Chinks of the World Machine: Feminism and Science Fiction.* London: Women's Press, 1988.

McGuirk, Carol. "The 'New' Romancers: Science Fiction Innovators from Gernsback to Gibson." *Fiction 2000: Cyberpunk and the Future of Narrative.* Eds. George E. Slusser and Tom Shippey. Athens: University of Georgia Press, 1992. 109-29.

Merrick, Helen. "Feminist/Science/Fictions: a case study of feminist cultural production in critical and popular communities." PhD Thesis. Perth: University of Western Australia, 1998.

Niven, Larry and Jerry Pournelle. *The Mote in God's Eye.* 1974. London: Macdonald Futura, 1980.

Nye, Andrea. *Feminist Theory and the Philosophies of Man.* 1988. London: Routledge, 1989.

Roberts, Robin. *A New Species: Gender and Science in Science Fiction.* Urbana: University of Illinois Press, 1993.

Schuyler, William M., Jr. "Sexes, Genders and Discrimination." *Erotic Universe: Sexuality and Fantastic Literature.* Ed. Donald Palumbo. New York: Greenwood, 1986.

Stone, Allucquere Rosanne. "*Risking Themselves*: Identity in Oshkosh." *The War of Desire and Technology at the Close of the Mechanical Age.* Cambridge, MA: MIT Press, 1995. 45-63.

Villani, Jim. "The Woman Science Fiction Writer and the Non-Heroic Male Protagonist." *Patterns of the Fantastic.* Ed. Donald M. Hassler. Mercer Island: Starmont House, 1983. 21-30.

Letterspace:
In The Chinks between
Published Fiction and Published Criticism

Correspondence between Lois Bujold and
Sylvia Kelso

Prologue: Sylvia Kelso

Going to WisCon20 (1996), I had almost finished
a PhD thesis on the interaction of feminist action and
theory with the work of a number of writers in Gothic
and science fiction. One of the SF writers was Lois
McMaster Bujold. Since I worked in a North Queensland town far from Australian SF writers, let alone US
conventions and the heart of fandom, my dissertation
was almost entirely text-based: I had never met any of
the people whose work I studied. WisCon 20 remedied
this in a truly spectacular fashion. I will long remember
looking out across my first-ever panel's audience to discover, seated in a back row with her customary look of
steely-eyed concentration, a face I instantly recognized
from cover photos and the interviews I had used in my

final thesis chapter: none other than Lois McMaster Bujold in the flesh.

WisCon 20's delirious atmosphere encouraged me not just to encounter "LMB" afterwards, but to talk at length with her: a true delight for a reader long bursting to harangue the unfortunate writer on just what about her work had been most exciting, and doubly so for an academic given the chance to test her theories against real-life data. Sometime during these encounters I rashly offered to send Lois copies of the academic work I had done on her fiction, and she, more rashly, accepted. The result was a letter sequence, part of which Helen (Merrick) and Tess (Williams) asked us to edit for their WisCon 20 anthology, *Women of Other Worlds* (1999).

The tradition of such exchanges between writer and reader, or just between interested literates, goes back to the European literary salons, which made letters a genre in their own right. Letters are also the oldest form of "informal criticism," to use Samuel R. Delany's term, which has been vital from the start of the SF community; to clone another of his terms, they are a paracritical form of paraliterary space. In shifting the old intellectual paradigm of authorless fiction handled in a public sphere by faceless criticism, they also move toward the personal/political merger so important to feminists. As published, these letters fit, but do not quite fit, all the above categories. They are not quite informal criticism, because they don't appear in a Letters column, nor yet quite formal criticism, because this is not an academic journal; they are not quite off-the-cuff comment because they are in print, nor yet quite official authorial statements, like an Afterword or Preface. Thus I hope they continue the blurring of public/private, high/low, academic/literary boundaries that has become so much a mark of feminist action, of science fiction, and for me, of WisCon 20 itself.

Letter 1: Sylvia Kelso to Lois Bujold

Dear Lois (McMaster Bujold),

(Without the bracket it still feels like *lèsè majeste*.)

You may or may not remember talking to me at length…at WisCon—a highlight of a memorable weekend, so far as I was concerned; anyhow, I am pretty sure (it WAS a frantic weekend) I said I'd send you the critical stuff I had done on your work, so I'm enclosing the pieces here…

"The Gernsback Continuum" is the final analytical chapter in my PhD; I did male and female pairs [of SF writers] who began writing at different periods or had different relations to feminism. You and Gibson were writers beginning in the '80s. Since the study's supposed to end at 1989, your later work got telescoped—in fact, I am pushing the boundaries, really, to deal with *Barrayar*; would have loved to do more on *Mirror Dance*… I would particularly like your input on this stuff at any point you don't think I've done you justice; you were somewhat short-sheeted on space anyway, since there's been so much more academic work on Gibson that I had to deal with.

[The chapter argued that, while William Gibson reacted against feminism and feminist SF, and hence ended back in the Boys' Own Stories to use Andrew Ross's term, of technological, masculinist SF, or the "Gernsback Continuum," LMB had "subsumed" feminism, in Joan Gordon's phrase, but was being pulled back into the "Continuum," despite her remarkable innovations, by her space opera plotlines, her young male protagonists, and reader and publishing demands for more of the same.]

…I could have written SO much more about [your characterization] which is very near to Le Guin's earlier crusades for character against technology or ideas, [and] to me the most innovative part of your work. [In particular, the chapter reads Miles Vorkosigan, LMB's long-standing protagonist, as codedly feminine in Robin Roberts' term: a male character who, as LMB herself discussed with Ken Lake, confronts women's problems like physical fragility, being regarded as deformed, and having to prevail by manipulation and wits.]

The [closing] comments on the future of the saga are open for your feedback. I thought of shoe-horning your point about being creatively exhausted after *Mirror Dance* in here, then pointing out that the need to write another book is in fact another facet of the Gernsback continuum,[1] but thought I would let you see how it looked pre-discussion.

The Section's [closure also ends] the SF part and the analytical body of the thesis. The implicit question throughout has been, How does feminism affect popular fictional forms? The answer involves my SF theory chapter, where I set SF up as a cyborg, a coupling together, in Haraway's specific theoretical framework, of forms and disciplines.

---

1   "The Gernsback Continuum" (1981) is a short story by William Gibson that points out the ongoing and alarming similarity of SF futures, based in the 1930s "golden age" of scientism, to the futures envisioned by Fascism."

[The final image of SF was as a Junk World, like the runaway space station in C.J. Cherryh's *Port Eternity*, that had assimilated feminism along with nearly everything else.]

Letter 2: Lois Bujold to Sylvia Kelso

Dear Sylvia,

Your big packet arrived yesterday, and I've read and thoroughly enjoyed it. I'd like to comment at length, but I'm dashing off tomorrow AM to the Science Fiction Research Conference in Eau Claire…

I will tolerate the description of Miles as "codedly feminine," but I note in passing that, judging from my fan mail and the people who turn up for my readings, my readership is divided, almost exactly and possibly uniquely, 50-50 among males and females… My own personal view is that men and women aren't two different things, just slight variations on the one thing, a view rooted in genetics, embryology, and my own experience. But many people—not just men—have a vested interest in claiming otherwise.

So if you figure Miles as codedly feminine, what d'you make of *Mark*, huh, huh?…

[On the] opening paragraph of my section [in the thesis]. Uh, yeah. I've noticed this disparity in outside attention between myself and Gibson… I'd be fascinated to hear your deconstructive analysis of *why* this should be so. Makes me a touch paranoid. Am I simply not the data they want to support their theories? My work does indeed remain hopelessly, stubbornly, mulishly in-genre...

I was very taken with your metaphor at the end, of SF as an aggregation. I like that a lot. Like Miles, it's not that we pick up so many women, it's that we never put any *down*...

I can hardly wait for you to read *Memory*. If it succeeds (in the artistic, not the financial sense) as I wish it to, it should throw a strong and interesting back-light over the whole of the previous series and Miles's character development therein. Your end-comment, re: "reader demand and the tradition's inertia are apparently beginning to push Bujold into the same mold" is so loaded with untested assumptions about how and why I work, I hardly know where to begin ripping it apart. That had better wait for my next letter...but if SF indeed is resisting destruction, all I can say is, Hurrah! Or, to coin a paraphrase, your post-modernist despair does not constitute my emergency.

Letter 3: Sylvia Kelso to Lois Bujold

Dear Lois,

[...]

Miles and codedly feminine and male and female approval...I don't think I brought out clearly...in the chapter...that a codedly feminine character doesn't preclude masculine/male identification at any point—C.J. Cherryh's male protagonists, for example, are perfect romance heroines: high-spirited but physically weak against powerful aliens (read men, even when female), given to fits of emotion shown subjectively, prevailing by a cross of moral courage and wilful disobedience (beginning to sound like anybody?). Yet C.J. Cherryh is the one female writer in a *Locus* survey who made the top-ten SF books you'd take to a desert island, and she's the writer Darko Suvin says he still follows now he no longer reads across the genre. I suspect that identification in a novel is a VERY shifty thing. As I understand it, the whole thing about gender differentiation [is that] gender constructions…are *constructions*—they do not fit everybody, and often don't fit anyone properly, and that's the problem—especially when those in power, as there always are, have a vested interest in maintaining them.

If Miles is codedly feminine, what'd I make of Mark? Ohhh boy, you really want me to say?!! I could bounce Mark off half a dozen theoretical approaches, including the biographical, using what you said to me about (I paraphrase) *Mirror Dance* being the story of your divorce… Far fairer is to read [him] as codedly feminine inside the cultural frame. Here I would say that Miles and Mark are Take One and Take Two: Miles is the acceptable version of Le Guin's man-woman—he does all the things women would LIKE to do—wins by wits and keeps charity, lacks muscles and still manages to manipulate, leads on battlefields and can "tie a knot and go on" better than Wellington himself. He's manic, intellectually brilliant, yet keeps compassion and sensitivity—he always feels for his dead, to begin with. For all his problems, though, Miles is the daylight version of the codedly feminine.

Mark is the night-time version—the codedly feminine that women DON'T like to face: to start with his body, he is forced into a shape that's not natural, and he has that eternal women's problem, weight—as [our mutual friend] Tess pointed out in her one-page take in her Masters…he even has a usually female eating disorder, bulimia. Also unlike Miles, he doesn't come good in the masculine gung-ho areas like leadership charisma and field-command abilities. And he suffers for most of the book from self-hate, hideously low self-esteem, and masochism… I've seen far too many friends go through those sort of guilt trips (yes, including over a divorce) to say they aren't prevalently women's problems. But there are a good few black Oedipal fantasies under there too—Mark kills Miles, and he nearly kills Aral. Is that wanting to kill your good self and your father, or what?

Again, Mark has the split personality that gets women locked up in little white rooms, Mark got the REALLY dirty childhood—and Mark gets to do the hate and rancor and envy that women aren't supposed to admit—either in the culture at large, among women, or often, even among feminists… But I think where Mark really taps into the night-time feminine is that Mark does what Miles physically can't—Mark kills… physically, hand-to-hand. And that is the one thing women really are socially pressured against… What is really interesting is that by being codedly feminine Mark sidesteps that whole acculturation, even while he's taking it to the max. Joanna Russ got heaps[2] for

---

2 Editor's note: This is an Australian idiom equivalent to the US "heaps of trouble."

Jael's killing in *The Female Man* (from women AND men AND feminists)—nobody turns a hair about Mark's number on the Baron in *Mirror Dance*, firstly because the guy deserves it, but secondly because it's done by a guy. I notice, actually, thinking back, that the veto on women's violence goes right through the Miles series to *Shards of Honour*...takes Cavilo to do it in cold blood. You could hardly call Mark's number cold-blooded, but there's a real pointer with that street-fight—that's when it first came home to this reader that Miles and Mark are different at the deepest point—that Mark can KILL.

So I have no problem at all with reading both Miles and Mark as codedly feminine...[b]ut I still think one of the things that powers *Mirror Dance* is this tapping into the real taboos of femalestuff. I also think that's where a lot of the creative draining AND the sense of an increase in power (which it does have, undoubtedly) are coming from. A lot of this stuff is really untracked, fictionally, and also psychically stressful territory...

Then there are Marxist approaches. If I did a deconstructive Marxist reading, a la Macherey, I'd need a lot more historical background; a Machereyan deconstruction goes, Where are the fractures and silences in this text, and to what contemporary historical situations do they relate? If I did that I would home in almost immediately on the empire of Barrayar—an empire in a decade of multinational corporations? On the colonial framework, also anachronistic, of endless unfettered expansion... Then, having been sensitized by doing Delany and Russ, I'd ask about sexualities—how come, in an era when alternate sexualities are more visible than they've ever been, the text's nearest approach is a few hints of sodomy (not a whisper of lesbianism) and the presence of a (spurned and narratively suppressed) hermaphrodite? Again, looking at the American background, I'd go, Where are the religious fundamentalists, and more forcefully, Where are the Hispanics, the Native Americans, and the Blacks? I might even read Mark's cloning as a convenient narrative way of dodging all these problems, just as the empire is a handy way to conceal the Vorkosigan capital.

If you read Mark through class patterns...in a more orthodox Marxist approach, then he's the upper-classes' *doppelganger*; that's why he haunts Cordelia, and Miles and Aral as well. If Miles is coming down off the aristocratic ladder, Mark's the devil climbing from the basement; he then functions as the embodiment of middle-class guilts, and the ending's a very pretty narrative solution (critspeak for a bandaid) that reconciles them to each other smack in the entrepreneurial middle-class...

I could [also] do a Marxist/feminist reading, and see Mark as the abused women's bodies that produce society's use-value (unpaid labour) with another bandaid solution where he's absorbed into the social order he's tried to escape—it's called reification and commodification of resistance to make it a resource, and boy, does Mark turn out to be that—and he even gets to pay for his crimes on the way through.

But enough of Mark, before you pitch the whole letter across the room. Going on to disparity in critical attention...I'd like to take this one with your final point about being glad that SF's resisting destruction. As I see it, there are two answers to, Why do you get skipped? Answer one, I only realised after I argued with a woman at WisCon…who said "Isn't she just about immature guys and things?" [That is], you don't fit the feminist SF critics' canon, because, (1) You usually have a male protagonist; (2) You don't do feminist Utopias; (3) You don't do alternate sexualities, and in especial lesbians, and (4) You aren't overtly politicized. I could add, although it's a pretty nebulous feeling, that you also don't do women's cyberpunk, which seems to be where a lot of critical attention is going at the moment…

Answer two, which is historically specific; as you saw in my chapter, in the '80s you're up against William Gibson. And…I have to admit it, the guy crystallized the information revolution and cyberculture, and *Neuromancer* has historical agency in a way I can't think of with any other SF text since *Dune*… So the cultural studies people and the technocultural historians focus on *Neuromancer*, because it's a historical land-mark—while the real-life cyberpunks also worship the guy. Then, in SF, *Neuromancer* processed a new topos, cyberspace or virtual reality, which is damn rare—a once in a lifetime book, and very few writers ever get near doing that… add that he gave it a cultural matrix…and is he going to pull SF critics' attention? And then, the guy had Bruce Sterling to bat for him…

Answer three (well, three answers) ties up with my lament at the end of the chapter… You…remark that "[my] post-modern despair is not [your] emergency" over the failure of feminism to transform SF. [But] SF was, has always been, and remains a genre principally written by guys for guys—the women that are in there are stellar, but they're fighting the inertia of the whole

Gernsback continuum…a masculinist bias that's culturally enforced—I have trouble getting students in Women in Literature courses to read something as soft as Connie Willis's *Uncharted Territory* because THEY see SF as something for guys, and they aren't interested. So women in SF are fighting both women's prejudice and the bias of the genre, its writers and its community…I had a collection of SF stories to review the other day, published 1996, going back to the 1890s…there were two, count them, two stories by women, and one was Ursula Le Guin's "Semley's Necklace," for Chrissake—and Connie Willis, with six…Nebulas for short fiction never even appeared… So my postmodern despair OUGHT to be your emergency, buen'amiga, because one of the reasons you are being ignored is that…you don't fit the male canon either in the community or the critical industry; so unless you catch their eyes with a sand-blaster like *Left Hand of Darkness*, the male academics are also gonna find you invisible…

End of the jeremiad. I (heavily underlined) can hardly wait to read *Memory* either, but at this rate, it won't be before 1997—we still don't have *Cetaganda*, even on the library shelves…

Letter 4: Lois Bujold to Sylvia Kelso

Dear Sylvia,

Thanks much for the spin on Mark, that's just what I wanted. So glad to know, after stuffing all that stuff into that book, that at least some readers are capable of pulling it all back out. And, er, more.

I most like the idea of Miles and Mark as day and night-time sides of the codedly feminine. They are, at any rate, drawn from day and night sides of *me*, though I'm not sure if I, personally, can stand as a Representative Female... I'm certainly not a Representative Male, or Representative Frog, though I would most prefer... to be a Representative Human... I was in a terribly gleeful mood, firing a lot of Mark onto the pages. I also had a strong sense of turning myself inside out; if there were any under-layers of my mind left unstripped to create him, they sure escape me.

I can relate the "killing your good self" spin directly to my divorce, and particularize it. I had pretty strong views on my marriage vows, and held myself to many less-than-wonderful years of wedded un-bliss on the grounds that I had taken an oath (remind you of anyone?). I still had an ideal of marriage, even though my particular sample fell short, and I was quite proud of how long mine had lasted... In order to escape at last, I had to kill my idealist-self—or at least freeze it and put it in a box for temporary storage—to let the self-interested self, the *selfish* self, save us all... As long as I was releasing the highly-inhibited selfish-self, why not go all the way and throw in the rest of the crew?... I had wonderful mad fun writing that book, once it

100

became at least inchoately apparent to me what I was doing. There are times when your Good Self just can't save you… (Did I also mention that Mark is going to end up a *very* rich man? And women are discouraged from paying attention to money, too…)

"Killing your father"… Hm, I don't think so. For one thing, Mark doesn't; it was [his handlers]' idea. Try this reading: killing the father in yourself is something women are encouraged to do when constructing their gender identity… Like Mark, I actually refused to kill my father—my masculine side (also my SF-reading side)—even though my handlers—society—put enormous pressure upon me to do so. (I just crippled it some)…

I don't know enough about deconstructive literary Marxism to react very intelligently to that spin.… Barrayar as the white-bread suburb of the galaxy? Maybe. Because it sidesteps all those current social problems is exactly why this world offers mental or emotional escape… One of the things which I would not expect to be apparent to you as an Australian is the degree to which the Dendarii District is a stand-in for West Virginia.

I have a fundamental problem with the concept of social class as applied to humans. Has anyone noticed that it does not denote anything real? People are completely mobile across class; there's not a damned thing about it that is inherent to individuals. And there's nothing but individuals really out there…the idea that classes are a kind of race, genetically inherited, is *very* nineteenth century. And British. And obsolete. Rather like craniometry…

The lines from your chapter that set me off on that rant about how and why I work were:…"reader demand and the tradition's inertia are apparently beginning to push Bujold back into the same mold."

I had a slew of reactions to that… Who says a work must have a female protagonist to be feminist? Who says reader demand compels what books I choose to write? Who says I *can* choose what I write?… Who says I gotta write feminist books at all?…

More considered reflection brings up this. While there are certainly feminist elements in my work… that phrasing…implies…that I am some sort of unconscious *gonfalonier* for feminism; that this constitutes an *agenda* for my work, an agenda which I am being discouraged from pursuing further by market pressure. But…in fact my work is driven by another agenda, a personal and psychological pursuit of an ongoing theme, personal identity, which sometimes but only sometimes intersects issues of feminism. So far from being discouraged from *that* theme, I am still pursuing it closely; *Memory* and the book planned to follow it (which may include a female viewpoint character) push it to my max.

I am not a political writer, which is perhaps another unfortunate—though undeniable—reason for my lack of academic attention. The politics portrayed in my works exist almost wholly to brace the psychological plot…and…are set around the problems of characterization, which are central; and I hope, more universal.

I write, in any given year, the book I can or must write. Some years I can bring a lot of energy and new knowledge to the task, and those years I'll manage one of the bigger theme books; other years I'll be running on empty, have to coast on my accumulated momentum while my engines re-charge…. In no case do I have much choice of theme; it chooses me. What's going on in the world around me leaks in, to be sure, so the game of detecting influences is not invalid; but it's what going on in the world *inside* me that makes the books. I do not and cannot write to market, whether that market be Star Wars or feminist academic politics…

Explorations of identity formation intersect problems of feminism in many areas… It's valid to say, as you do, that I incorporate many feminist concerns. The notion that I have "accumulated" feminism, like SF itself does, is quite nice; but I feel I have *assimilated* science fiction itself…it really is part of my identity, to the point where I can turn around a[nd] generate it again out of the deepest recesses of my being. I *like* the idea that I might be part of "the Gernsback continuum" (if by that you mean the whole of SF, and not just its masculinist biases), that I might both embody and exemplify it… Why not view both masculinism and feminism as part of the accumulation, instead of one as the necessary annihilator of the other?

(Practical answer: because at the moment, masculinism still holds a disproportionate number of the marbles, I suppose, yeah, all right, can't argue there. I'm doing my best to turn that around, y'know. Can a personal example of a successful woman indeed not change the rules of the game?…)

Hm. I'm being suckered in, here, by the fascination of your arguments, out of my proper position. *I* am the data; *you* are the theorist. It's your job to explain things.

It's my job to be myself, at the top of my form. A good theorist starts with the data, and then constructs the theories round them…any theory of SF must now account for me. I don't, thank God, have to account for myself…

But what I was trying to get at with the "Your postmodernist despair" line was simply that NOBODY tells me what to write. Not the genre, not, certainly, hostile critics of the genre, not my family nor friends nor feminists (nor masculinists).… (The "your" in that line was construed by me to mean "Gibson, the Movement, et al." not "Sylvia Kelso," by the way…I think it should have been phrased "*Their* post-modernist despair does not constitute my emergency.") Nor my agenda. My own inner psychological need to explore a particular theme, lately growing clearer to me in the way it parallels developments in my own psyche, has sent me down a particular narrative road, and I simply haven't got to the end yet. When I do, I'll stop, and do something else…

I do know the trick will be done with the Miles books, though. My friend Pat Wrede ran an experiment when I was developing one of the recent novels…if I really wrote for theme, as I claimed, why not transplant the theme to another set of characters and setting, and proceed with my psyche-spinning just the same? I tried the idea. Didn't work. It had to be Miles. It's possible that I've invested so much emotional weight in Miles, I can no longer escape his orbit, but that's not the *tradition's* inertia.

It does mean also that I'm incapable of changing what I write in order to go whoring after academic attention, which is probably a good thing in the long run. What we need to do instead is to change *them*…

I really must stop; it's too seductively fun to write about writing instead of actually writing… That's quite enough stuff to dump on a working woman!

Letter 5: Sylvia Kelso to Lois Bujold

Dear Lois,

THIS time I am gonna respond while the iron is hot, my shoulder to the wheel and my nose to the ground…

Interesting that you relate the killing of good self directly to your divorce, 'cause originally I wrote you a paragraph that did just that—then I thought, this is no fair using of personal communication and chopped it… No wonder you had great fun writing Mark—talk about exercising the black gang…whee! (Did I tell you we—my black-gang and I—have appropriated black-gang as a name for the Brownies as Stevenson called 'em—the non-conscious part of the creative process, if you wanna be stuffy.) Yeah, I forgot to mention that Mark's money-making proclivities are also "un-feminine"—and unaristocratic, of course…

Social class as nineteenth century, British, and obsolete. Oh, how I wish. Yeah, people are mobile across 'em, but they are there.… I thought it didn't exist in Oz till I read John Fiske's breakdown of shops in Sydney Centrepoint—lower class bright, junky, and in the street, middle class bright, well-price-signed, inside the shop, high-class upstairs, windows almost empty, no price signs—and found I ALWAYS went for the middle-class ones. I only have to read Stephen King's novels and see how often the minor villains are lower class, and I somehow don't think it's obsolete in the US either. Maybe more invisible, but obsolete?…

OK, more serious answer to your comments… about the thesis closure line: (1) Q. You said "Who says work must have female protag. to be feminist?" A. Not me, lady, I said Miles was codedly feminine—although most overtly feminist texts do seem to go for female protagonists, it's not prescriptive, at least not for me.

(2) Q. Who says reader demand compels what books I choose to write? A. Mmm. "Reader demand" here also covers publishing criteria, etc.… I seem to remember you yourself writing that *Warrior's Apprentice* got your toe in the publisher's door—not *Shards*, which is (in my opinion) a far less Gernsbackish book—I can imagine old Hugo tucking *Apprentice* into the early *Astounding* no trouble—no way could I see him taking *Shards*—too much "woman" in it.

(3) Q. Who says you can choose what you write? A. Well, from what I gather, beyond the creative imperatives, publishers and editors and what they perceive as market pressures have quite a lot of say in it. Didn't you also say to me you did *Cetaganda* 'cause you were contracted?

Further down page—no, I do not consider you an unconscious *gonfalonier* for feminism; nor do I think you have it as an agenda. Nobody has had feminism as an agenda in SF since about 1976… However, I do find that one of the most fascinating and elusive aspects of '80s work [in any field] is the way feminist discourse and feminist stances turn up, apparently naturalized, and people use [them] without consciously having an agenda… I am quite sure that your work is driven by a personal agenda; what interests me is the points where your work and feminist stuff intersect.

Probably, I guess, the writer-as-person got edited out of the equation; as you said in the library speech, a book isn't complete till the reader completes it, so from the academic view, what matters is the reader-response and the text. And an academic reading is just an over-empowered reader response. So your book (even if You wrote it) and my "your book" (even if I'm just reading it) are not always the same thing… (The tendency to talk about "Bujold" as shorthand for "the work published under LMB's name" is also partly responsible for this reading, I have no doubt.) And if you have a female viewpoint in post-*Memory*, great…!

You are not out of your proper position to respond to my arguments in kind; your work may be my data, but I would like to think you are also a person and in dialogue, and therefore we can squeak about things that interest both about some work that (at this point) just happens to be yours. I like bouncing ideas off real minds almost as much (more?) than I do working out theories to fit data output by such minds…

Really interesting that themes won't transfer away from Miles. Maybe you really are in his orbit (is there a Trojan point in there?)… As a writer, I tend to go, Hey, you aren't writing themes, you're writing people… Here's a cute question— What starts your books? An idea? A question? A sentence? A dream? A scene? A seed image? Le Guin said LHOD started with the seed image of two people with a sledge on snow. Shelley said *Frankenstein* started with a dream. What kicks yours off?

Letter 6: Lois Bujold to Sylvia Kelso

Dear Sylvia,

Since everything I wanted to say about your concluding comments in your thesis about where my series seems to be going kept ending up, "But wait till you read *Memory*!" I finally decided it would be easier if you just *read* the blasted book. So I've sent you a copy, via air mail parcel… After poring endlessly over all the drafts, galleys, and the final product, I've concluded I don't really want to read that book any more, what I want is for someone *else* to read it…

The main reason I don't want to join in the fascinating game of SF literary criticism is that I don't have *time*…even in the little dabbling I've done, I've discovered it eats thinking and writing time (and energy) like a sonofabitch. Too *much* fun. I'll just have to save it for a retirement hobby…

"What starts my books." Never dreams, as far as I know. Images, yes, for sure. The first image I had of *The Warrior's Apprentice* was of Bothari getting his chest blown out in defense of Miles, before I knew anything else about the books. That image took place on a shuttleport tarmac, and I knew nothing about the assailants. The real scene…was much mutated. Much of my writing consists of inspiration linked by logic; I have certain scenes I'm writing toward, like emotional peaks sticking up out of a foggy landscape, and the road to be traveled in between has to be figured out by a combination of logic and panic…

I did have one short story that began with a sentence, which hung around in a notebook for some time till I thought of a story to run in under it. "Her pancakes were all running together in the center of the griddle, like conjugating amoebas." It became the opening line of "Barter," my first sale…

Letter 7: Sylvia Kelso to Lois Bujold

Dear LMB,

Where do I start? Bells, whistles, Hallelujah chorus… Delighted? Honoured? Charmed?…(flattered to all hell?)… anyway—short version: GEE WHIZ—THANKS!…

I will torment you by doing the small stuff first. It's a great read, as usual—a nail-chewer, if not QUITE as horrendous as the middle of *Mirror Dance*… It's nice to have Illyan turned into a person, and it's a neat ET riff on the mole spy-story—shades of [LeCarré's] *Tinker Tailor Soldier Spy* all over the place, and of course paranoia is home country on Barrayar… [But] this one really felt like the closure of a series, with that recapitulation/resolution pattern, finally releasing Elena, going back to and leaving Silvy Vale, ta-ta foreshadowed for Taura, bye-bye Quinn, bye-bye the Dendarii…

Okay, next the nasties. I almost had a heart attack at the beginning when Miles was holding forth about Imperial auditors and Laisa was going "Yes, yes" and I thought, Sheesh, LMB hasn't fallen into that SF guy thing where men lecture and women listen, SURELY? On second read, I knew the logistical reason for the Auditor explanation, but first time through I really went Ouch…

Final and nastiest nasty, and I will have to get back to this with *Cetaganda*, because I'm still thinking through the extraordinarily complex gender politics of the haut ladies—the thing I did NOT like here was the way the women got sidelined: what got up my nose worst is the scene at the Residence where Cordelia and Laisa and I think Alys have to scarf off so the guys can talk business. Even first time through, when I was in full forward momentum with Miles's Illyan Crusade and ImpSec cockroach hunt, that REALLLLLY niggled me.

I would guess, getting down to the real bottom of the scumbag, that… I think I'm getting impatient to SEE gender change on Barrayar. We had Drou as a female bodyguard and Cordelia and Kareen changing the course of Empire back in *Barrayar*—how come we are now back to women as aid and comfort stations and satellites? Yeah, I know Alys kicks butt to start the Illyan rescue, and Raina's mother is changing Silvy Vale, and Laisa has a business doctorate—how much use is that gonna be when her greatest occupation is remembering how the Imperial Auditor and Old Family Bunjie (Oz for mate) takes his coffee? I guess I'm just plain greedy. I want Miles and I want Utopia as well. When are women gonna have some POWER?

No doubt you think this is a scurvy return for your magnificent gesture, and it is; but I would be supping with Haroche if I didn't say what I honestly think.

HOW-ever, to finish the scum tour... I think I would be prepared, once I get the extraordinarily fascinating knot of the haut dames straightened out, to argue of both *Cetaganda* and *Memory* that despite your arguments...buen'amiga (sheesh, maybe not after this, she thought) these two actually bear out my hypothesis...because even if we take Miles as codedly feminine, these books are sidelining women as did not happen in *Barrayar*—in fact, with those palace byplays at the end of *Memory*... AND the assertion of the emperor's rightness at the end of *Cetaganda*, they are heading women right back for their traditional place...

Now for the good bits. For Miles, logistically and...a whole lot of otherwise, the Imperial Auditor thing is an absolute stroke of GENIUS. Sets him loose to go on being Vorkosigan-Naismith without perpetually having to do the *enfant terrible*, always bucking his command chain...—re-opens space...even without the Dendarii, gives him an even better chance to grow up and stop playing soldiers. And I think that step out of the warrior's apprentice perspective is the most exciting thing about the book.

Then we start digging deeper on the Miles front, and first there's a repeat, it appears, of the Mark personae-reconciliation. I guess Naismith was so deeply entrenched it took both you AND Miles two books to kill him off, hey? I have to admit to considerable nostalgia... There was a certain first fine careless rapture about *Warrior's Apprentice*, in particular, that I still adore, and which is, of course, as I myself pointed out way back in "Continuum," unsustainable for a series without ossifying the guy.

OTOH, as they say on the email, it looks like Naismith didn't so much get killed…as subsumed—I mean, Ivan sees him come out at the start of the Auditorship. I am not sure if these are confused or complex signals, since Miles pretty definitely refers to Naismith later as being dead; OTOH, that-idiot-Ivan has a habit of occasionally hitting the bullseye dead-on… I would PREFER to see Naismith as not subsumed so much as integrated; kind of like Mark's black-gang… This is an interesting move when Miles is read as codedly feminine and Naismith as Vorkosigan's double, because, as I can't remember if I have remarked to you before, while women don't kill their male characters' doubles, they DO kill female ones—viz. Bronte with Bertha in *Jane Eyre* for the most famous case… For the academic reading, therefore, there is a nice balance of, does Miles kill Naismith, in which case we have *Jane Eyre* in undress greens, or does Miles integrate Naismith, in which case postmodernists have a problem with regression to the old humanist-masculinist dream of a single, unfractured identity?

I must admit there's a strong sense of that happening whether Naismith is killed or integrated; Miles gets to the still point of the turning world and he chooses "to be me." Whatever the hell that is. I am hoping that…it will turn out to be any number of things. Which gives me to consider that this may be a women's (generic) advantage. Women are expected to be a number of things from astro-cartographer to mother—men who flip through a number of careers are tacitly taken to be light and frivolous. I confess to an interest in the folded, fractured, and shuffled multiple personality, like eluki bes shahar's Butterfly, who at the end of her trilogy has half the villain's memories in a clone of his daughter's body, and says she is "who I will be in the next minute." My postmodern aesthetic hankering for wildly open and resistant endings does great warfare with my romantic's desire to see it all end happily over THAT one… So in one way the end of *Memory*, with Miles as captain of his soul, is absolutely satisfactory, and in another it's not… I guess this is a transit book, really. Miles grows up…from the point of view of the military SF genre and the tradition of the male adolescent-type space opera protagonist, this is a *coup de force*—for Miles, it's what you hinted to me, a growth out beyond *Mirror Dance*, yeah, carried unanimously, I love it. From these other niggly perspectives…I'm gonna be a goddamn Oliver. I still want more….

I hope the stuff on *Memory* is not too scurvy a return for your princely gift… Oh! The sacking scene with Illyan was a crackerjack. I got to the end and just had to put the book down and go "Sheez…"

In less inarticulate terms, it was enormously powerful and totally devastating. How's that for a back-page blurb?

Letter 8: Lois Bujold to Sylvia Kelso

Dear Sylvia,

I'm glad you're enjoying *Memory*, and even more glad you've found *Cetaganda*. Upon reflection, I realized *Cetaganda* may give you more stuff to chew upon, from a feminist-scholar viewpoint, than I thought; I tend to dismiss it as a minor book because...Miles does not undergo any profound psychological changes in it. Do note, as a series prequel, the plot is intrinsically required to return to the *status ante quo* [sic] at the end... This is, upon experiment and reflection, the main reason I shall be avoiding prequels in future. I want my characters to have free will, and the ability to effect change, and a prequel is locked in a deterministic universe...

Your nasties were bearable, truly. I have a writer's group whose whole job is to point out as much of this stuff as possible, so I'm used to it...

Re: the data dump conversation about Imperial Auditors... When Miles takes center stage, *everyone* gets sidelined. If you compare Miles and Laisa in this scene, you are comparing a major with a minor character. Properly, you should compare her with Galeni, a character of equal weight. In this scene, Laisa speaks 17 times, Galeni speaks once.

In the scene where...Galeni is being arrested, well, that's Barrayar for you... The coffee scene likewise. If Barrayar wasn't sexist as all hell, Miles would have a galactic wife by now. If I made Barrayar progress too quickly towards feminist utopia, I'd just have to go invent *another* Planet of the Patriarchy to have the proper conflict...and to have the deck suitably stacked against my characters. Besides, my universe already has an egalitarian utopia, Beta Colony. Let's try for some cultural diversity, eh?

Beneath your complaint are a couple of other assumptions. The plea for demonstrated steps toward feminist utopia…is in part assuming that what I write, because it is labeled SF, is some sort of futurism… It's nothing of the sort. I write psychological allegory, actually a sly sort of fantasy with technology… I don't think Miles's future is realistically possible in any way, starting with faster than light travel. It's a sort of high-tech middle-earth.

But even or especially if it is psychological allegory, do I therefore have a moral duty to provide fictional role-models for women? Who says so? What benefit, to escape all the "shoulds" of tradition, merely to replace them with another equally constraining set of radical "shoulds"? I have no desire merely to replace a Patriarchy with a Matriarchy, thanks. Each is equally prone to slip into toxic, soul-destroying forms…

Where has anyone experienced a matriarchy for test-comparison? you may logically ask. In fact, most of us have, as children. When the scale of our whole world was one block long, it was a world dominated and controlled by women. Who were twice our size, drove cars, had money, could hit us if they wanted to and we couldn't ever hit them back… Hence, at bottom, my deep, deep suspicion of feminism, matriarchy, etc. Does this mean putting my mother in charge of the world, and me demoted to a child again? No thanks, I'll pass…

This leads me to another thought—give me a couple of minutes here, and I'll probably argue my way back to your position after all. Women do desperately need models for power other than the maternal. Nothing is more likely to set any subordinate's back up, whether they be male or female, than for their boss to come the "mother knows best" routine at them... We need a third place to stand. I'm just not clear how it became my job to supply it.

Your plea for more active female characters is a good one, though. Happily we will be able to test this thesis...with *Ekaterin* (next book, working title), which is structured to evenly split the viewpoint between Miles and a Barrayaran lady named Ekaterin Nile Vorsoisson. With the viewpoint distributed more even-handedly, you will better be able to tell how much sidelining of female characters is due to viewpoint selection, and how much is due to intrinsic biases...

Ekaterin is my first attempt in a while to write a really female character, from the inside out, and it's extraordinarily uncomfortable. She's Barrayaran Vor from a very traditional background, about Miles's age, and on the verge of...her first mid-life crisis, you know, the one where you discover that everything they told you was wrong... I do think that another aspect of male viewpoint characters for both female writers and readers is the *escape* it offers from one's female human condition. What, then, of the psychology of those female readers who feel gender-restricted to read only women's books (e.g., certainly not SF, or only feminist SF?)...

Miles talks about Naismith's "death," but in fact it only feels that way to him because he's a bit depressed and tends to self-dramatization (oh, you noticed?). Miles's growth in *Memory* was costly, make no mistake… There will always be sadness and nostalgia for what he's lost—no accident, that the last scene of the book is him getting drunk in an empty room… But he will have absolutely no desire to go back… When once you've got bigger, it's very hard ever to get smaller again.

No "*Jane Eyre* in undress greens" (great line); Miles has not killed Naismith, exactly… I guess I'd say Miles *repossessed* Naismith. Integrated is not quite so nicely accurate a term. Repossessed is perfect. Miles as psychological repo-man. Guess the little admiral didn't keep up the payments…

Letter 9: Sylvia Kelso to Lois Bujold

Dear LMB,

Yeah, *Cetaganda* is in many ways more interesting for a gender analysis than *Memory*, which is more riveting to the devoted Miles-reader. (When did you decide on Miles for his name, btw? VERY Latin-literate; how many people comment on it?) I know what you mean about the plot being cramped by predestination, have had occasion to observe the iron hand of prequels in action before, most notably with Zimmer Bradley's *Darkover* series. OTOH, the haut ladies are truly charming to the feminist critic because 1. They're on the bad side, but 2. It appears they are being given credit for farsighted and intelligent behavior and even power, although 3. It's pretty difficult to let 'em have too much power without their shanghaiing the story out from under Miles, while 4. It's just as hard to keep Miles from turning them from Wicked Witches to Damsels in Distress. I liked the whole interaction with the Star Créche and consorts and thought it was a pity the emperor had to haul 'em back in line. Why couldn't the new Empress have decided the strat. was faulty for herself?...

BUT, still contesting the data-dump Imperial Auditor's conversation, I am well used to Miles sidelining everybody—I will never forget my first experience in *Apprentice*—but usually, he doesn't talk quite so much in quite such an orthodox data-dump fashion, and it's not so completely addressed to the female, whether she talks or not...

"That's Barrayar for you," Planets of the Patriarchy, cultural diversity. It's precisely that it is Barrayar that I'm niggling about; why does it have to stay Patriarchal?... Why can't conflicts take place during the process of change? And yeah, your universe has Beta Colony, but we've never been there except passing through—and when Cordelia went home, which pretty smartly turned it into a critical utopia—so why, indeed, can't we have cultural diversity? Take me to Beta Colony, LMB, I'd LOVE to see more than the Silicon Zoo!...

All that sounded remarkably contentious. Take it as voice of agitating reader and not prescriptive critic. "Demonstrated steps toward feminist utopia"—nah, I don't want that, if I want feminist utopias I read [Marge Piercy's] *Woman on the Edge of Time*—nor do I see why you have to be predictive and prescriptive. I'm not urging you to a moral duty…as a reader I just want you to do me some more women like Cordelia and Drou!

I think SF can be futurism, but there's absolutely no reason why it has to be… And I don't want fictional role models—what use as a role model would I find a female mercenary—on second thought, don't answer that, I know the insides of academe! I do want women I can enjoy reading about. I spent my early SF reading guys' versions of strong or tough or funny women; nowadays, with rare exceptions like John Varley's *Titan*, I can't take the flavor any more. I don't necessarily want 'em to be politically correct, and I don't always want Utopias, but I do want my SF to have women up front, and women who are as good as guys if not better, and what, for want of a better word, I guess, I would call a woman-flavor to the writing. Which your stuff always had to me, or I wouldn't still be reading it.

Third nit-pick. Why should the "shoulds" of Patriarchal tradition have to be replaced by those of a Matriarchy? I want somewhere where men and women balance the power between 'em—… And anyway, why should a feminist utopia be a matriarchy? Again, see *Woman on the Edge of Time*. But you can have great women characters without anything like a feminist utopia—what about C.J. Cherryh's *Rimrunners* or her Hani series or Janet Kagan's *Hellspark* or Denise Lopez Heald's *Mistwalker*, to name just the stuff I can see on my shelves? Oh, wow, again this is starting to sound contentious. OK, score background inflection as tone of mild argument…

But again…who says feminist utopias have to equal matriarchies? To me as a heterosexual and probably some sort of liberal, they would be mutually exclusive terms. I write [fictional] matriarchies, quite often, for the pleasure of imaginatively turning the tables on guys, but almost as soon as I do, I start to pull them down. OTOH, I don't write patriarchies because I have the goddamn thing right here in real life—I guess that covers the question of escape from the female human condition. I'm not interested, anymore, in escaping to a male viewpoint. I'm interested in escaping to a world where a woman's viewpoint is good…. But I definitely agree that women need more power role models… As for it being your job to supply the "third place for women to stand," though—hey, I can write 'em for myself if I want, and I do. It isn't your job, it's just my demand…

Ekaterin sounds deeply interesting… I suppose viewpoint selection might be an intrinsic bias; but going on Le Guin's and McKee Charnas's testimony… it seems more likely to be cultural. The norm seems to be to start with a male viewpoint as being "easier." Le Guin actually said she needed feminism to write women, and Charnas says she had hell with Alldera in *Walk*… But what do you consider constitutes a really "female" character?

I guess Fiametta [from LMB's *The Spirit Ring*] would be her nearest foremother, from the split viewpoint angle; but why is it uncomfortable? This is really odd, esp. considering how comfortably Cordelia comes over in *Shards* and *Barrayar*. Do you figure it's because you are setting E. up in the same story as Miles? If Miles is codedly feminine, the same problem might pertain as with Mark—you can only have one of them "up" while the other one is "down"… Or is it because E.'s trad[itional] Barrayaran and Cordelia is a Betan Utopist?

Letter 10: Lois Bujold to Sylvia Kelso

Dear Sylvia,

Yes, my email has arrived![3] We can now continue this conversation much more, er, conversationally. Workloads permitting…

This letter is mainly to convey the new email address, but I'll hit a few spots in yours…

I stole the name Miles from Miles Hendron, from Mark Twain's *The Prince and the Pauper*… At the time, I was innocent of the Latin connection, but I bet Twain wasn't. I was very pleased when I found out. I also found after the fact that "vor" means thief in Russian and that Barrayar can be approximately translated as "bleak valley." Insert "Twilight Zone" background music here.

I very much liked your line, "I'm interested in escaping to a world where the woman's viewpoint is good."…

Ekaterin is an uncomfortable character to write at present, in part because she's in a terribly uncomfortable situation, highly constrained in a traditional role. Cordelia was always autonomous, or at least knew she was there by her own choice. Things should ease a bit as the novel progresses and Ekaterin's situation changes, but not before she goes though a great deal of the hell I've scheduled for her. I'm now at the end of Ch. 6, contemplating Ch. 7. A looong way to go to completion…

---

3   LMB has just acquired an email account.

Epilogue: Sylvia Kelso

And since the dialogue has shifted to email, this seems a good place to follow feminist tradition, which considers closures something of a masculinist device, and read the exchange as a (temporarily) isolated episode rather than a completed unit. If a last line is needed, it might, perhaps, be drawn from that other SF tradition, the longrunning TV series: Even though we pause here, "The truth is (still) out there somewhere…"

Author Biography

Sylvia Kelso is an adjunct lecturer at James Cook University of North Queensland, Australia. She has a PhD on feminism(s), SF, and the Gothic, and has published on SF, fantasy, horror, and the creative writing process, in *Science Fiction Studies*, *Journal for the Fantastic in the Arts*, *Foundation*, *Paradoxa: Journal of Literary Genres*, *Femspec*, and *The New York Review of Science Fiction*. She recently guest edited a special volume of Paradoxa on Ursula K. Le Guin. Her novels *The Moving Water* and *Amberlight* were short-listed for best fantasy novel in the 2007 and 2008 Aurealis Australian genre fiction awards.